SPANISH
Essential Language for Short Trips
FAST TALK

Fast Talk Spanish
2nd edition – March 2009 First published – May 2004

Published by
Lonely Planet Publications Pty Ltd ABN 36 005 607 983
90 Maribyrnong St, Footscray, Victoria 3011, Australia

Lonely Planet Offices
Australia Locked Bag 1, Footscray, Victoria 3011
USA 150 Linden St, Oakland CA 94607
UK 2nd Floor, 186 City Road, London ECV1 2NT

Photography
Casa Mila by Mauritius Images/Rene Mattes

ISBN 978 1 74104 228 3

text © Lonely Planet Publications Pty Ltd 2004

10 9 8 7 6 5 4 3 2

Printed by Hang Tai Printing Company
Printed in China

Mixed Sources
Product group from well-managed
forests and other controlled sources
www.fsc.org Cert no. SGS-COC-005002
© 1996 Forest Stewardship Council

CHAT 6

EXPLORE 13

SHOP 20

ENJOY 25

EAT & DRINK 27

SERVICES 44

GO 48

SLEEP 56

WORK 60

HELP 62

LOOK UP 67

Language name: Spanish

Spanish is known to its native speakers as both *español*, es·pa·*nyol*, and *castellano*, kas·te·*lya*·no.

Language family: Romance

Spanish belongs to the Romance family of languages and is a close relative of both Italian and Portuguese.

Key country & secondary countries:

Spanish is spoken not only in Spain but in many other countries all over the world. It's the language of most of Latin America and the West Indies as well as parts of Africa, the Phillipines, Guam and the USA, making it one of the world's most widely spoken languages.

Approximate number of speakers:

There are some 390 million speakers of Spanish worldwide.

Donations to English:

English has borrowed numerous words from Spanish, including alligator, bonanza, canyon, guerilla and chocolate. Many of these borrowings are in turn derived from the indigenous languages of Latin America.

Grammar:

The structure of Spanish holds no major surprises for English speakers because the two languages are closely related.

Pronunciation:

Many Spanish sounds are similar to those found in English, so English speakers won't find making themselves understood in Spanish difficult.

Abbreviations used in this book:

m	masculine	sg	singular	pol	polite
f	feminine	pl	plural	inf	informal

CHAT
Meeting & greeting

Hello/Hi.	*Hola.*	*o*·la
Good morning.	*Buenos días.*	*bwe*·nos *dee*·as
Good afternoon. (until 8pm)	*Buenas tardes.*	*bwe*·nas *tar*·des
Good evening.	*Buenas noches.*	*bwe*·nas *no*·ches
See you later.	*Hasta luego.*	*as*·ta *lwe*·go
Goodbye./Bye.	*Adiós.*	a·*dyos*
How are you?	*¿Cómo está(s)?* pol/inf	*ko*·mo es·*ta(s)*
Fine, thanks.	*Bien, gracias.*	byen *gra*·thyas
Mr	*Señor*	se·*nyor*
Sir	*Don*	don
Ms/Mrs	*Señora*	se·*nyo*·ra
Madam	*Doña*	*do*·nya
Miss	*Señorita*	se·nyo·*ree*·ta

Essentials

Yes.	*Sí.*	see
No.	*No.*	no
Please.	*Por favor.*	por fa·*vor*
Thank you (very much).	*(Muchas) Gracias.*	(*moo*·chas) *gra*·thyas
You're welcome.	*De nada.*	de *na*·da
Excuse me.	*Perdón/Discúlpeme.*	per·*don*/dees·*kool*·pe·me
Sorry.	*Lo siento.*	lo *syen*·to

What's your name?
¿Cómo se llama Usted? pol	*ko*·mo se *lya*·ma oos·*te*
¿Cómo te llamas? inf	*ko*·mo te *lya*·mas

My name is ...
Me llamo ...	me *lya*·mo ...

I'd like to introduce you to ...
Quisiera presentarle a ... pol	kee·*sye*·ra pre·sen·*tar*·le a ...
Quisiera presentarte a ... inf	kee·*sye*·ra pre·sen·*tar*·te a ...

I'm pleased to meet you.
Mucho gusto.	*moo*·cho *goos*·to

It's been great meeting you.
Me ha encantado conocerle. pol	me a en·kan·*ta*·do ko·no·*ther*·le
Me ha encantado conocerte. inf	me a en·kan·*ta*·do ko·no·*ther*·te

This is my ... *Éste/a es mi ...* m/f *es*·te/a es mee ...
child	*hijo/a* m/f	*ee*·kho/a
colleague	*colega* m&f	ko·*le*·ga
friend	*amigo/a* m/f	a·*mee*·go/a
husband	*marido* m	ma·*ree*·do
partner (intimate)	*pareja* m&f	pa·*re*·kha
wife	*esposa* f	es·*po*·sa

I'm here ... *Estoy aquí ...* es·*toy* a·*kee* ...
for a holiday	*de vacaciones*	de va·ka·*thyo*·nes
on business	*en viaje de negocios*	en *vya*·khe de ne·*go*·thyos
to study	*estudiando*	es·too·*dyan*·do
with my family	*con mi familia*	kon mee fa·*mee*·lya
with my partner (intimate)	*con mi pareja*	kon mee pa·*re*·kha

How long are you here for?
¿Cuánto tiempo le va a quedar? pol	*kwan*·to *tyem*·po le va a ke·*dar*
¿Cuánto tiempo te vas a quedar? inf	*kwan*·to *tyem*·po te vas a ke·*dar*

I'm here for ... days/weeks.
Estoy aquí por ... días/ es·*toy* a·*kee* por ... *dee*·as/
semanas. se·*ma*·nas

For numbers, see the box feature in **LOOK UP,** page 67.

Here's my ...	*Ésta es mi ...*	es·ta es mee ...
What's your ...?	*¿Cuál es su/tu ...?* pol/inf	kwal es soo/too ...
address	*dirección*	dee·rek·*thyon*
email address	*dirección*	dee·rek·*thyon*
	de email	de ee·mayl
fax number	*número de fax*	*noo*·me·ro de faks
home number	*número de*	*noo*·me·ro de
	teléfono	te·*le*·fo·no
mobile number	*número de*	*noo*·me·ro de
	móvil	*mo*·veel
work number	*número de*	*noo*·me·ro de
	teléfono en el	te·*le*·fo·no en el
	trabajo	tra·*ba*·kho

Breaking the language barrier

I speak a little Spanish.
Hablo un poco de español. *ab*·lo oon *po*·ko de es·pa·*nyol*

Do you speak English?
¿Habla inglés? *ab*·la een·*gles*

Does anyone speak English?
¿Hay alguien que hable inglés? ai al·*gyen* ke *ab*·le een·*gles*

Do you understand?
¿Me entiende? me en·*tyen*·de

I (don't) understand.
(No) Entiendo. (no) en·*tyen*·do

How do you pronounce this word?
¿Cómo se pronuncia   *ko·*mo se pro·*noon·*thya
esta palabra?   es·ta pa·*lab·*ra

How do you write 'ciudad'?
¿Cómo se escribe 'ciudad'?   *ko·*mo se es·*kree·*be theew·*da*

What does ... mean?
¿Qué significa ...?   ke seeg·nee·*fee·*ka ...

Could you repeat that?
¿Puede repetir?   *pwe·*de re·pe·*teer*

Could you please ...?   *¿Puede ..., por favor?*   *pwe·*de ... por fa·*vor*
    speak more   *hablar más*   ab·*lar* mas
    slowly   *despacio*   des·*pa·*thyo
    write it down   *escribirlo*   es·kree·*beer·*lo

Personal details

Where are you from?
¿De dónde es/eres? pol/inf   de *don·*de es/*e·*res

I'm from ...   *Soy de ...*   soy de ...
    Australia   *Australia*   ow·*stra·*lya
    Canada   *Canadá*   ka·na·*da*
    England   *Inglaterra*   een·gla·*te·*ra
    the USA   *los Estados*   los es·*ta·*dos
             Unidos   oo·*nee·*dos

I'm ...   *Estoy ...*   es·*toy* ...
    married   *casado/a* m/f   ka·*sa·*do/a
    separated   *separado/a* m/f   se·pa·*ra·*do/a
    divorced   *divorciado/a* m/f   dee·vor·*thya·*do/a

I'm single.
Soy soltero/a. m/f   soy sol·*te·*ro/a

9

Occupations & study

What do you do?

¿A qué le dedica? pol		a ke le de·*dee*·ka
¿A qué te dedicas? inf		a ke te de·*dee*·kas

I'm a/an ...	*Soy ...*	soy ...
architect	*arquitecto/a* m/f	ar·kee·*tek*·to/a
teacher	*profesor/*	pro·fe·*sor/*
	profesora m/f	pro·fe·*so*·ra
mechanic	*mecánico/a* m/f	me·*ka*·nee·ko/a
writer	*escritor/*	es·kree·*tor/*
	escritora m/f	es·kree·*to*·ra

I work in ...	*Trabajo en ...*	tra·*ba*·kho en ...
education	*enseñanza*	en·se·*nyan*·tha
hospitality	*hostelería*	os·te·le·*ree*·a
sales & marketing	*ventas y*	*ven*·tas ee
	marketing	mar·ke·teen

I'm ...	*Estoy ...*	es·*toy* ...
retired	*jubilado/a* m/f	khoo·bee·*la*·do/a
unemployed	*en el paro*	en el *pa*·ro

I'm studying ...	*Estudio ...*	es·*too*·dyo ...
business	*comercio*	ko·*mer*·thyo
languages	*idiomas*	ee·*dyo*·mas
science	*ciencias*	*thyen*·thyas

What are you studying?

¿Qué estudia? pol		ke es·*too*·dya
¿Qué estudias? inf		ke es·*too*·dyas

For other occupations, see the dictionary in **LOOK UP**, page 70.

Age

How old ...?	¿Cuántos años ...?	kwan·tos a·nyos ...
are you	tiene/tienes pol/inf	tye·ne/tye·nes
is your daughter	tiene su/tu hija pol/inf	tye·ne soo/too ee·kha
is your son	tiene su/tu hijo pol/inf	tye·ne soo/too ee·kho

I'm ... years old.
Tengo ... años.   ten·go ... a·nyos

He/She is ... years old.
Él/Ella tiene ... años.   el/e·lya tye·ne ... a·nyos

For your age, see the numbers box in **LOOK UP**, page 67.

Feelings

I'm ...	*Tengo ...*	ten·go ...
I'm not ...	*No tengo ...*	no ten·go ...
Are you ...?	*¿Tiene/Tienes ...?* pol/inf	tye·ne/tye·nes ...
cold	*frío*	free·o
hot	*calor*	ka·lor
hungry	*hambre*	am·bre
in a hurry	*prisa*	pree·sa
thirsty	*sed*	se

I'm ...	*Estoy ...*	es·toy ...
I'm not ...	*No estoy ...*	no es·toy ...
Are you ...?	*¿Está/Estás ...?* pol/inf	es·ta/es·tas ...
annoyed	*fastidiado/a* m/f	fas·tee·dya·do/a
embarrassed	*avergonzado/a* m/f	a·ver·gon·tha·do/a
tired	*cansado/a* m/f	kan·sa·do/a
well	*bien*	byen

Beliefs

I'm (not) ...	(No) Soy ...	(no) soy ...
agnostic	agnóstico/a m/f	ag·nos·tee·ko/a
Buddhist	budista	boo·dees·ta
Catholic	católico/a m/f	ka·to·lee·ko/a
Christian	cristiano/a m/f	krees·tya·no/a
Hindu	hindú	een·doo
Jewish	judío/a m/f	khoo·dee·o/a
Muslim	musulmán/	moo·sool·man/
	musulmána m/f	moo·sool·ma·na
practising	practicante	prak·tee·kan·te
religious	religioso/a m/f	re·lee·khyo·so/a

Weather

What's the weather like?
¿Qué tiempo hace?   ke *tyem*·po *a*·the

(Today) It's raining.
(Hoy) Está lloviendo.   (oy) es·ta lyo·vyen·do

(Today) It's snowing.
(Hoy) Nieva.   (oy) nye·va

Today it's ...	Hoy hace ...	oy a·the ...
Will it be ...	¿Mañana hará ...?	ma·nya·na a·ra ...
tomorrow?		
cold	frío	free·o
freezing	un frío que pela	oon free·o ke pe·la
hot	calor	ka·lor
sunny	sol	sol
warm	calor	ka·lor
windy	viento	vyen·to

EXPLORE
Doing the sights

Do you have information on local places of interest?
¿Tiene información   *tye*·ne een·for·ma·*thyon*
sobre los lugares   *so*·bre los loo·*ga*·res
de interés local?   de een·te·*res* lo·*kal*

I have (one day).
Tengo (un día).   *ten*·go (oon *dee*·a)

Can we hire a guide?
¿Podemos alquilar un guía?   po·*de*·mos al·kee·*lar* oon *gee*·a

I'd like to see ...
Me gustaría ver ...   me goos·ta·*ree*·a ver ...

What's that?
¿Qué es eso?   ke es *e*·so

Who made it?
¿Quién lo hizo?   kyen lo *ee*·tho

How old is it?
¿De qué época es?   de ke *e*·po·ka es

I'd like a/an ...   *Quisiera ...*   kee·*sye*·ra ...
   audio set   *un equipo audio*   oon e·*kee*·po *ow*·dyo
   catalogue   *un catálogo*   oon ka·*ta*·lo·go
   guidebook in   *una guía*   *oo*·na *gee*·a
    English   *turística*   too·*rees*·tee·ka
     en inglés   en een·*gles*
   (local) map   *un mapa*   oon *ma*·pa
     (de la zona)   (de la *tho*·na)

Could you take a photograph of me?
¿Me puede/puedes hacer   me *pwe*·de/*pwe*·des a·*ther*
una foto? pol/inf   *oo*·na *fo*·to

Can I take photographs (of you)?
¿(Le/Te) Puedo   (le/te) *pwe*·do
tomar fotos? pol/inf   to·*mar fo*·tos

I'll send you the photograph.
Le/Te mandaré la foto. pol/inf   le/te man·da·*re* la *fo*·to

Gallery & museum hopping

When's the ... open? *¿A qué hora abre ...?*   a ke *o*·ra *a*·bre ...
   gallery   *la galería*   la ga·le·*ree*·a
   museum   *el museo*   el moo·*se*·o

What's in the collection?
¿Qué hay en la colección?   ke ai en la ko·lek·*thyon*

What kind of art are you interested in?
¿Qué tipo de arte   ke *tee*·po de *ar*·te
le/te interesa? pol/inf   le/te een·te·*re*·sa

I'm interested in ...
Me interesa/interesan ... sg/pl   me een·te·*re*·sa/een·te·*re*·san ...

What do you think of ...?
¿Qué piensa/piensas de ...? pol/inf   ke *pyen*·sa/*pyen*·sas de ...

It's a/an exhibition of ...
Es una exposición de ...   es *oo*·na eks·po·see·*thyon* de ...

I like the works of ...
Me gustan las obras de ...   me *goos*·tan las *o*·bras de ...

It reminds me of ...
Me recuerda a ...   me re·*kwer*·da a ...

... art   *arte ...*   *ar*·te ...
   graphic   *gráfico*   *gra*·fee·ko
   Impressionist   *Impresionista*   eem·pre·syo·*nees*·ta
   Modernist   *Modernista*   mo·der·*nees*·ta
   Renaissance   *renacentista*   re·na·then·*tees*·ta

Getting in

What time does it open?
¿A qué hora abren? a ke *o*·ra *ab*·ren

What time does it close?
¿A qué hora cierran? a ke *o*·ra *thye*·ran

What's the admission charge?
¿Cuánto cuesta la entrada? *kwan*·to *kwes*·ta la en·*tra*·da

It costs (seven Euros).
Cuesta (siete Euros). *kwes*·ta (*sye*·te e·oo·ros)

Is there a discount for …?	*¿Hay descuentos para …?*	ai des·*kwen*·tos *pa*·ra …
children	*niños*	*nee*·nyos
families	*familias*	fa·*mee*·lee·as
groups	*grupos*	*groo*·pos
pensioners	*pensionistas*	pen·syo·*nees*·tas
students	*estudiantes*	es·too·*dyan*·tes

Tours

Can you recommend a …?	*¿Puede recomendar algún/alguna …?* m/f	pwe·de re·ko·men·*dar* al·*goon*/al·*goo*·na …
boat trip	*paseo* m *en barca*	pa·*se*·o en *bar*·ka
excursion	*excursión* f	eks·koor·*syon*
tour	*recorrido* m	re·ko·*ree*·do

When's the next …?	*¿Cuándo es el/la próximo/a …?* m/f	*kwan*·do es el/la *prok*·see·mo/a …
boat trip	*paseo* m *en barca*	pa·*se*·o en *bar*·ka
excursion	*excursión* f	eks·koor·*syon*
tour	*recorrido* m	re·ko·*ree*·do

15

Do I need to take ... with me?	¿Necesito llevar ...?	ne·the·*see*·to lye·*var* ...
Is ... included?	¿Incluye ...?	een·*kloo*·ye ...
accommodation	el alojamiento	el a·lo·kha·*myen*·to
the admission charge	el precio de entrada	el *pre*·thyo de en·*tra*·da
equipment	equipo	e·*kee*·po
food	comida	ko·*mee*·da
transport	transporte	trans·*por*·te

Can we hire a guide?
¿Podemos alquilar un guía? po·*de*·mos al·kee·*lar* oon *gee*·a

The guide will pay.
El guía va a pagar. el *gee*·a va a pa·*gar*

The guide has paid.
El guía ha pagado. el *gee*·a a pa·*ga*·do

Do I need to take (lunch) with me?
¿Necesito llevar (el almuerzo)? ne·the·*see*·to lye·*var* (el al·*mwer*·tho)

How long is the tour?
¿Cuánto dura el recorrido? *kwan*·to *doo*·ra el re·ko·*ree*·do

What time should I be back?
¿A qué hora tengo que volver? a ke *o*·ra *ten*·go ke vol·*ver*

Be back here at ...
Vuelva a ... *vwel*·va ...

I'm with them.
Voy con ellos. voy kon e·*lyos*

I've lost my group.
He perdido mi grupo. e per·*dee*·do mee *groo*·po

Have you seen a group of (Australians)?
¿Ha visto un grupo de (Australianos)? a *vees*·to oon *groo*·po de (ow·stra·*lya*·nos)

Top 6 day trips

Sometimes the frenzied pace of Barcelona and Madrid can get a little overwhelming. For a more relaxing alternative, head out of town to enjoy a quieter, off-the-beaten-track cultural experience.

Barcelona

Montserrat   mont·se·rat

This remarkable massif of limestone pinnacles rising over deep gorges is also the spiritual heart of Catalonia. Thousands of people visit the Monastery of Montserrat each year to venerate the statue of *La Moreneta* (the Black Virgin).

Sitges   seet·ges

This seaside resort town is a summertime mecca for fashionable city folk and a huge international gay set. In the 1890s it was a trendy bohemian hang-out and it has remained one of Spain's most unconventional resorts.

Teatre-Museu Dalí   te·a·tre moo·se·oo da·lee

Situated at Figueres, Dalí's birthplace, the museum comprises three floors of tricks, illusions and absurdities which allow the visitor to wander through one of the most fertile imaginations of the 20th century.

Madrid

Real Palacio de Aranjuez   re·al pa·la·thyo de a·ran·khweth

Once a royal playground, this vast and richly decorated palace and its meticulously maintained gardens make a popular weekend getaway.

San Lorenzo de El Escorial   san lo·ren·tho de el es·ko·ryal

Sheltering at the foot of the Sierra de Guadarrama this magnificent 16th century complex consisting of a huge monastery, royal palace and mausoleum is a must-see. Among the artistic riches on display are a crucifix by Benvenuto Cellini and paintings by El Greco, Titian, Tintoretto and Bosch.

Toledo   to·le·do

Situated on a hilltop in a bend of the River Tajo, Toledo is a remarkably beautiful city. It's a treasure trove of architectural history with its labyrinthine medieval streets, alcazar (Moorish fortified palace) and stunning cathedral.

Top 10 sights

It would take a lifetime to explore all the wonders of the vibrant arts and culture of both Barcelona and Madrid. If you don't have that much time on your hands, make sure you pack in a few of these famous highlights:

Barcelona

Fundación Joan Miró   foon·da·*syon zho*·an mee·*ro*

The largest single collection of the painter Joan Miró's work is housed in a magnificent building designed by his friend Josep Luís Sert. The combination of natural light, white walls and airy galleries make this a wonderful setting to appreciate the works of Catalonia's greatest artist.

La Sagrada Família   la sa·*gra*·da fa·*mee*·lya

Designed by Gaudí, this half-complete church with its soaring towers and detailed, textured facades is emblematic of Barcelona and is the most visited unfinished building site in the world. This colossal edifice takes up a whole block of the l'Eixample district and has its own metro station.

Manzana de la Discordia   man·*sa*·na de la dees·*kor*·dya

This remarkable stretch of Passeig de Gràcia is called the 'Block of Discord', because you'll find wildly contrasting works of the three greatest architects of Modernisme on it. Domènech i Montaner, Puig i Cadafalch and Gaudí were hired by the city's most well-heeled families to have their houses remodelled in the hip new style.

Palau de la   pa·*low* de la
Música Catalana   moo·see·ka ka·ta·*la*·na

This concert hall is one of Barcelona's most brilliant highlights and is celebrated by many as the crowning glory of Modernisme. The bare brick facade of mosaics, tile-clad pillars and busts only hints at the richness of the decoration of the interior. The auditorium is a splendid symphony of ceramics and stained glass.

Parc Güell   park goo·el

The park where Gaudí turned his hand to landscape gardening is one of the most wonderful on the planet – a jovial and enchanting spot to relax. Gaudí's inimitable style has created a place where the artificial almost seems more natural than the endeavours of Mother Nature. The park contains a wonderful esplanade, the centrepiece of which is the Banc de Trencadis, a delightful bench that curves around its perimeter and is clad with ceramics.

Madrid

Campo del Moro   kam·po del mo·ro

This exquisite park laid out in the English style was once a playground for royal children. Among the greenery you'll find winding paths, verdant canopies, neatly laid-out flower beds, fountains and wandering peacocks.

Museo del Prado   moo·the·o del pra·do

The staggering richness of the Museo del Prado's collection is a reason in itself for many people to come to Madrid. Its three floors are packed with masterpieces with the works of Spanish masters El Greco, Goya and Velasquez featuring prominently.

Palacio Real   pa·la·thyo re·al

This vast Italianate palace, commenced by Felipe V, comprises some 2800 rooms, 50 of which are open to the general public. The interiors are a marvel of sumptuous decoration.

Plaza de la Villa   pla·tha de la vee·lya

Thought to have been the city's permanent seat of government in the Middle Ages, this square is one of Madrid's most beautiful spots, with a sense of history and some fine architecture including the 15th century Casa de los Lujanes.

Plaza Mayor   pla·tha ma·yor

The imperial heart of Madrid beats loudest at this town square. Once the site of royal festivities, bullfights and autos-da-fé (the ritual condemnation and burning of herectics) it's now given over to those fancying an alfresco drink or snack, or wanting to rendezvous in an obvious location.

19

SHOP
Essentials

Where's ...?	¿Dónde está(n) ...? sg/pl	don·de es·ta(n) ...
a bank	un banco sg	oon ban·ko
a department store	unos grandes almacenes pl	oo·nos gran·des al·ma·the·nes
a supermarket	un supermercado sg	oon soo·per·mer·ka·do

Where can I buy ...?
¿Dónde puedo comprar ...?   don·de pwe·do kom·prar ...

I'd like to buy ...
Quisiera comprar ...   kee·sye·ra kom·prar ...

I'm just looking.
Sólo estoy mirando.   so·lo es·toy mee·ran·do

Can I look at it?
¿Puedo verlo?   pwe·do ver·lo

Do you have any others?
¿Tiene otros?   tye·ne o·tros

Could I have a bag, please?
¿Podría darme una bolsa, por favor?   po·dree·a dar·me oo·na bol·sa por fa·vor

Could I have it wrapped?
¿Me lo podría envolver?   me lo po·dree·a en·vol·ver

Does it have a guarantee?
¿Tiene garantía?   tye·ne ga·ran·tee·a

Can I have it sent overseas?
¿Pueden enviarlo por correo a otro país?   pwe·den en·vee·ar·lo por ko·re·o a o·tro pa·ees

Can I pick it up later?
　　¿Puedo recogerlo más tarde?　　pwe·do re·ko·*kher*·lo mas *tar*·de

It's faulty.
　　Es defectuoso.　　es de·fek·too·*o*·so

I'd like ..., please.	*Quisiera ...,* *por favor.*	kee·*sye*·ra ... por fa·*vor*
my money back	*que me devuelva* *el dinero*	ke me de·*vwel*·va el dee·*ne*·ro
to return this	*devolver esto*	de·vol·*ver es*·to

Hot shop spots

Shopping in Spain is a retail revelation. Barcelona reportedly boasts the highest number of shops per person in Europe. Madrid, too, is a shopper's paradise with everything from tiny specialist stores to mammoth malls. In both cities it's the quality that impresses most.

Barri Gòtic, Barcelona – groovy street, club & second-hand wear • antique shops • quirky speciality shops

El Raval, Barcelona – design & fashion outlets • alternative clothes & music

La Ribera, Barcelona – artisan workshops

l'Eixample, Barcelona – local & international boutiques • jewellery stores

Chueca, Madrid – an excellent shopping precinct with fashionable shops

Plaza Mayor, Madrid – gifts • items typical of Madrid

Salamanca, Madrid – similar to Chueca but with more expensive, conservative tastes catered for

Paying

How much is this?
¿Cuánto cuesta esto? kwan·to kwes·ta es·to

Can you write down the price?
¿Puede escribir el precio? pwe·de es·kree·beer el pre·thyo

That's too expensive.
Es muy caro. es mooy ka·ro

I'll give you ...
Le daré ... le da·re ...

Do you have something cheaper?
¿Tiene algo más barato? tye·ne al·go mas ba·ra·to

Can I have smaller notes?
¿Me lo puede dar en me lo pwe·de dar en
billetes más pequeños? bee·lye·tes mas pe·ke·nyos

I'd like my change, please.
Quisiera mi cambio, por favor. kee·sye·ra mee kam·byo por fa·vor

Do you accept ...?	*¿Aceptan ...?*	a·thep·tan ...
credit cards	*tarjetas de crédito*	tar·khe·tas de kre·dee·to
debit cards	*tarjetas de débito*	tar·khe·tas de de·bee·to
travellers cheques	*cheques de viajero*	che·kes de vya·khe·ro
Could I have a ..., please?	*¿Podría darme ..., por favor?*	po·dree·a dar·me ... por fa·vor
bag	*una bolsa*	oo·na bol·sa
receipt	*un recibo*	oon re·thee·bo

Clothes & shoes

I'm looking for ...	Busco ...	boos·ko ...
jeans	vaqueros	va·ke·ros
shoes	zapatos	tha·pa·tos
underwear	ropa interior	ro·pa een·te·ryor

small	pequeña	pe·ke·nya
medium	mediana	me·dya·na
large	grande	gran·de

Can I try it on?
¿Me lo puedo probar? me lo pwe·do pro·bar

My size is (42).
Uso la talla (cuarenta y dos). oo·so la ta·lya (kwa·ren·ta ee dos)

It doesn't fit.
No me queda bien. no me ke·da byen

Books & music

Is there a/an	¿Hay algún/	ai al·goon/
(English-	alguna ...	al·goo·na ...
language) ...?	(en inglés)? m/f	(en een·gles)
book by ...	libro m de ...	lee·bro de ...
bookshop	librería m	lee·bre·ree·a
entertainment guide	guía f del ocio	gee·a del o·thyo
section	sección f	sek·thyon

I'd like (a) ...	Quisiera ...	kee·sye·ra ...
blank tape	una cinta	oo·na theen·ta
	virgen	veer·khen
CD	un cómpact	oon kom·pakt
headphones	unos	oo·nos
	auriculares	ow·ree·koo·la·res

23

I'd like (a) ...	Quisiera ...	kee·sye·ra ...
map	un mapa	oon ma·pa
newspaper	un periódico	oon pe·ryo·dee·ko
(in English)	(en inglés)	(en een·gles)
some paper	papel	pa·pel
pen	un bolígrafo	oon bo·lee·gra·fo
postcard	una postal	oo·na pos·tal

I heard a band called ...

Escuché a un grupo
que se llama ...

es·koo·che a oon groo·po
ke se lya·ma ...

What's their best recording?

¿Cuál es su mejor disco?   kwal es soo me·khor dees·ko

Can I listen to this?

¿Puedo escuchar este aquí?   pwe·do es·koo·char es·te a·kee

Photography

I need ... film for this camera.	Necesito película ... para esta cámara.	ne·the·see·to pe·lee·koo·la ... pa·ra es·ta ka·ma·ra
APS	APS	a pe e·se
B&W	en blanco y negro	en blan·ko y ne·gro
colour	en color	en ko·lor
(400) speed	de sensibilidad (cuatrocientos)	de sen·see·bee·lee·da (kwa·tro·thyen·tos)

How much is it to develop this film?

¿Cuánto cuesta revelar
este carrete?

kwan·to kwes·ta re·ve·lar
es·te ka·re·te

When will it be ready?

¿Cuándo estará listo?   kwan·do es·ta·ra lees·to

ENJOY
What's on?

What's on …?	¿Qué hay …?	ke ai …
locally	en la zona	en la *tho*·na
this weekend	este fin de semana	*es*·te feen de se·*ma*·na
today	hoy	oy
tonight	esta noche	*es*·ta *no*·che

Where are …?	¿Dónde hay …?	*don*·de ai …
gay venues	lugares gay	loo·*ga*·res ge
places to eat	lugares para comer	loo·*ga*·res *pa*·ra ko·*mer*
pubs	pubs	poobs

Is there a local … guide?	¿Hay una guía … de la zona?	ai *oo*·na *gee*·a … de la *tho*·na
entertainment	del ocio	del *o*·thyo
film	de cine	de *thee*·ne

I feel like going to a …	Tengo ganas de ir …	*ten*·go *ga*·nas de eer …
ballet	al ballet	al ba·*le*
bar	a un bar	a oon bar
cafe	a un cafe	a oon ka·*fe*
concert	a un concierto	a oon kon·*thyer*·to
karaoke bar	a un bar de karaoke	a oon bar de ka·ra·*o*·ke
nightclub	a una discoteca	a *oo*·na dees·ko·*te*·ka
party	a una fiesta	a *oo*·na *fyes*·ta
restaurant	a un restaurante	a oon res·tow·*ran*·te

Meeting up

What time shall we meet?
¿A qué hora quedamos?   a ke o·ra ke·*da*·mos

Where will we meet?
¿Dónde quedamos?   *don*·de ke·*da*·mos

Let's meet ...	*Quedamos ...*	ke·*da*·mos ...
at (eight) o'clock	*a (las ocho)*	a (las o·cho)
at the (entrance)	*en (la entrada)*	en (la en·*tra*·da)

Small talk

I (don't) like ...	*(No) Me gusta ...*	(no) me *goos*·ta ...
dancing	*ir a bailar*	eer a bai·*lar*
films	*el cine*	el *thee*·ne
music	*la música*	la *moo*·see·ka
pub crawls	*ir de bar en bar*	eer de bar en bar
shopping	*ir de compras*	eer de *kom*·pras

Do you like to ...?	*¿Le/Te gusta ...?* pol/inf	le/te *goos*·ta ...
go to concerts	*ir a conciertos*	eer a kon·*thyer*·tos
listen to music	*escuchar*	es·koo·*char*
	música	*moo*·see·ka
sing	*cantar*	kan·*tar*

I (don't) like ...	*(No) Me gusta/ gustan ...* sg/pl	(no) me *goos*·ta/ *goos*·tan ...
animated films	*películas* pl *de dibujos animados*	pe·*lee*·koo·las de dee·*boo*·khos a·nee·*ma*·dos
horror movies	*cine* sg *de terror*	*thee*·ne de te·*ror*
sci-fi films	*cine* sg *de ciencia ficción*	*thee*·ne de *thyen*·thya feek·*thyon*

EAT & DRINK

breakfast	desayuno m	de·sa·*yoo*·no
lunch	almuerzo m	al·*mwer*·tho
dinner	cena f	*the*·na
snack	tentempié m	ten·tem·*pye*
eat	comer	ko·*mer*
drink	beber	be·*ber*

Choosing & booking

Can you recommend a ...?	¿Puede recomendar un ...?	*pwe*·de re·ko·men·*dar* oon ...
bar	bar	bar
cafe	cafe	ka·*fe*
restaurant	restaurante	res·tow·*ran*·te
Where would you go for ...?	¿Adónde se va para ...?	a·*don*·de se va *pa*·ra ...
a celebration	celebrar	the·le·*brar*
a cheap meal	comer barato	ko·*mer* ba·*ra*·to
local specialities	comer comida típica	ko·*mer* ko·*mee*·da *tee*·pee·ka
I'd like ..., please.	Quisiera ..., por favor.	kee·*sye*·ra ... por fa·*vor*
the (non) smoking section	(no) fumadores	(no) foo·ma·*do*·res
a table for (five)	una mesa para (cinco)	*oo*·na *me*·sa *pa*·ra (*theen*·ko)

27

Eateries

Restaurants have been part of Spanish culture for centuries and you'll find a diverse selection of fantastic places to eat. Sample the local flavours at some of these eateries:

horno asador   *or·no a·sa·dor*

the quintessential Spanish restaurant centered around a massive wood-fired meat-roasting oven that imparts an atmospheric glow and an aroma to set carnivorous taste buds on fire

terraza   *te·ra·tha*

an alfresco restaurant, often with a small interior dining room, usually found clustered together with other *terrazas* (offering very similar menus) in city centres

restaurante   *res·tow·ran·te*

a proper sit-down restaurant much like any other in the Western world except that in Spain they tend to be small and intimate and more of a social institution

casa de comidas   *ka·sa de ko·mee·das*

a working-class restaurant that serves cheap, wholesome meals with excellent service

tasca   *tas·ka*

a tapas bar, sometimes the bar of a proper restaurant, where you can expect to find a lively atmosphere and a counter groaning with aromatic, mouth-watering self-serve tapas

jamónería   *kha·mon·e·ree·a*

a shrine to the Spanish passion for ham, the interior of this, ironically, seafood restaurant is festooned with countless legs of sweet-smelling ham which are consumed as appetisers

Ordering

What would you recommend?
¿Qué recomienda?   ke re·ko·*myen*·da

Please bring ...	*Por favor nos trae ...*	por fa·*vor* nos *tra*·e ...
the bill	*la cuenta*	la *kwen*·ta
the drink list	*la lista de*	la *lees*·ta de
	bebidas	be·*bee*·das
the menu	*el menú*	el me·*noo*
I'd like it ...	*Lo quiero ...*	lo *kye*·ro ...
medium	*no muy hecho*	no mooy e·cho
rare	*vuelta y vuelta*	*vwel*·ta ee *vwel*·ta
steamed	*al vapor*	al va·*por*
well-done	*muy hecho*	mooy e·cho
with the dressing	*con el aliño*	kon el a·*lee*·nyo
on the side	*aparte*	a·*par*·te
with/without ...	*con/sin ...*	kon/seen ...

Nonalcoholic drinks

(cup of) coffee ...	*(taza de) café* m ...	(*ta*·tha de) ka·*fe* ...
(cup of) tea ...	*(taza de) té* m ...	(*ta*·tha de) te ...
with milk	*con leche*	kon *le*·che
with/without sugar	*con/sin azúcar*	kon/seen a·*thoo*·kar
(orange) juice	*zumo* m *de (naranja)*	*zoo*·mo de (na·*ran*·kha)
soft drink	*refresco* m	re·*fres*·ko
... water	*agua* f ...	*a*·gwa ...
boiled	*hervida*	er·*vee*·da
(sparkling)	*mineral*	mee·ne·*ral*
mineral	*(con gas)*	(kon gas)

Alcoholic drinks

beer	*cerveza* f	ther·*ve*·tha
brandy	*coñac* m	ko·*nyak*
champagne	*champán* m	cham·*pan*
cocktail	*combinado* m	kom·bee·*na*·do
sangria (red- wine punch)	*sangría* f	san·*gree*·a

bottle/glass	*botella/copa* f	bo·*te*·lya/*ko*·pa
of … wine	*de vino …*	de *vee*·no …
dessert	*dulce*	*dool*·the
red	*tinto*	*teen*·to
rosé	*rosado*	ro·*sa*·do
sparkling	*espumoso*	es·poo·*mo*·so
white	*blanco*	*blan*·ko

… of beer	*… de cerveza*	… de ther·*ve*·tha
glass	*caña* f	*ka*·nya
jug	*jarra* f	*kha*·ra
pint	*pinta* f	*peen*·ta

| shot of (whisky) | *chupito* m *de (güisqui)* | choo·*pee*·to de (*gwees*·kee) |

In the bar

I'll have …
  Para mí …   pa·ra mee …

Same again, please.
  Otra de lo mismo.   o·tra de lo *mees*·mo

I'll buy you a drink.
  Le/Te invito a una copa. pol/inf   le/te een·*vee*·to a *oo*·na *ko*·pa

What would you like?
    ¿Qué quiere(s) tomar? pol/inf   ke *kye*·re(s) to·*mar*

It's my round.
    Es mi ronda.   es mee *ron*·da

How much is that?
    ¿Cuánto es eso?   *kwan*·to es *e*·so

Cheers!
    ¡Salud!   sa·*loo*

Buying food

How much is (a kilo of cheese)?
    ¿Cuánto vale   *kwan*·to *va*·le
    (un kilo de queso)?   (oon *kee*·lo de *ke*·so)

What's the local speciality?
    ¿Cuál es la especialidad   kwal es la es·pe·thya·lee·*da*
    de la zona?   de la *tho*·na

What's that?
    ¿Qué es eso?   ke es *e*·so

I'd like ...	*Póngame ...*	*pon*·ga·me ...
(200) grams	*(doscientos)*	(dos·*thyen*·tos)
	gramos	*gra*·mos
(two) kilos	*(dos) kilos*	(dos) *kee*·los
(three) pieces	*(tres) piezas*	(tres) *pye*·thas
(six) slices	*(seis) lonchas*	(seys) *lon*·chas
that one	*ése/a* m/f	*e*·se/a
two	*dos*	dos

Less, please.   *Menos, por favor.*   *me*·nos por fa·*vor*
Enough, thanks.   *Basta, gracias.*   *ba*·sta *gra*·thyas
More, please.   *Más, por favor.*   mas por fa·*vor*

Special diets & allergies

Is there a (vegetarian) restaurant near here?
¿Hay un restaurante   ai oon res·tow·*ran*·te
(vegetariano) por aquí?   (ve·khe·ta·*rya*·no) por a·*kee*

I'm vegetarian.
Soy vegetariano/a. m/f   soy ve·khe·ta·*rya*·no/a

I'm vegan.
Soy vegetariano/a   soy ve·khe·ta·*rya*·no/a
estricto/a. m/f   es·*treek*·to/a

I don't eat (red meat).
No como (carne roja).   no *ko*·mo (*kar*·ne *ro*·kha)

Could you prepare a meal without …?	*¿Me puede preparar una comida sin …?*	me *pwe*·de pre·pa·*rar oo*·na ko·*mee*·da seen …
butter	*mantequilla*	man·te·*kee*·lya
eggs	*huevo*	*we*·vo
fish	*pescado*	pes·*ka*·do
meat/ fish stock	*caldo de carne/ pescado*	*kal*·do de *kar*·ne/ pes·*ka*·do
pork	*cerdo*	*ther*·do
poultry	*aves*	*a*·ves

I'm allergic to …	*Soy alérgico/a …* m/f	soy a·*ler*·khee·ko/a …
dairy produce	*a los productos lácteos*	a los pro·*dook*·tos *lak*·te·os
eggs	*a los huevos*	a los *we*·vos
MSG	*al glutamato monosódico*	al gloo·ta·*ma*·to mo·no·*so*·dee·ko
nuts	*a las nueces*	a las *nwe*·thes
seafood	*a los mariscos*	a los ma·*rees*·kos
shellfish	*a los crustáceos*	a los kroos·*ta*·thyos

On the menu

Aperitivos	a·pe·ree·*tee*·vos	appetisers
Caldos	*kal*·dos	soups
De Entrada	de en·*tra*·da	entrées
Ensaladas	en·sa·*la*·das	salads
Segundos Platos	se·*goon*·dos *pla*·tos	main courses
Postres	*pos*·tres	desserts
Cervezas	ther·*ve*·thas	beers
Licores	lee·*ko*·res	spirits
Refrescos	re·*fres*·kos	soft drinks
Vinos Blancos	*vee*·nos *blan*·kos	white wines
Vinos Dulces	*vee*·nos *dool*·thes	dessert wines
Vinos Espumosos	*vee*·nos es·poo·*mo*·sos	sparkling wines
Vinos Tintos	*vee*·nos *teen*·tos	red wines
Digestivos	dee·khes·*tee*·vos	digestifs

For more help reading the menu, see the **Menu decoder** below.

Menu decoder

a la plancha	a la *plan*·cha	grilled • on a griddle
a la vasca	a la *vas*·ka	in a Basque green sauce
aceite m	a·*they*·te	oil
aceitunas f pl	a·*they·too*·nas	olives
— *rellenas*	re·*lye*·nas	stuffed olives
acelgas f pl	a·*thel*·gas	chard (a variety of beet)
adobo	a·*do*·bo	battered
aguacate m	a·gwa·*ka*·te	avocado
ahumado/a m/f	a·oo·*ma*·do/a	smoked
ajo m	a·kho	garlic
al ajillo	al a·*khee*·lyo	in garlic
al horno	al *or*·no	baked

albaricoque m	al·ba·ree·*ko*·ke	apricot
albóndigas f pl	al·*bon*·dee·gas	meatballs
alcachofa f	al·ka·*cho*·fa	artichoke
allioli m	a·*lyo*·lee	garlic sauce
almejas f pl	al·*me*·khas	clams
almendra f	al·*men*·dra	almond
alubias f pl	a·*loo*·byas	kidney beans
anchoas f pl	an·*cho*·as	anchovies
anguila f	an·*gwee*·la	eel
anís m	a·*nees*	anise
apio m	*a*·pyo	celery
arroz m	a·*roth*	rice
— *con leche*	kon *le*·che	rice pudding
asado/a m/f	a·*sa*·do/a	roasted
atún m	a·*toon*	tuna
bacalao m	ba·ka·*low*	salted cod
beicon m *con queso*	*bey*·kon kon *ke*·so	cold bacon with cheese
berberechos m pl	ber·be·*re*·chos	cockles
berenjena f	be·ren·*khe*·na	aubergine • eggplant
besugo m	be·*soo*·go	bream
bistec m	bee·*stek*	steak
— *con patatas*	kon pa·*ta*·tas	steak & chips
blanco m	*blan*·ko	white
bocadillo m	bo·ka·*dee*·lyo	tapas in a sandwich
bollos m pl	*bo*·lyos	bread rolls
boquerones m pl	bo·ke·*ro*·nes	anchovies
— *en vinagre*	en vee·*na*·gre	anchovies in vinaigrette
boquerones m pl *fritos*	bo·ke·*ro*·nes *free*·tos	fried anchovies
brasa	*bra*·sa	chargrilled
buey m	bwey	ox
butifarra f	boo·tee·*fa*·ra	thick sausage
cabra f	*ka*·bra	goat
cacahuete m	ka·ka·*we*·te	peanut

café m	ka·*fe*	coffee
— *con leche*	kon *le*·che	coffee with milk
— *cortado*	kor·*ta*·do	coffee with a little milk
— *descafeinado*	des·ka·fey·*na*·do	decaffeinated coffee
— *helado*	e·*la*·do	iced coffee
— *solo*	*so*·lo	black coffee
calabacín m	ka·la·ba·*theen*	courgette • zucchini
calabaza f	ka·la·*ba*·tha	pumpkin
calamares m pl	ka·la·*ma*·res	calamari • squid
— *a la romana*	a la ro·*ma*·na	calamari • squid rings fried in butter
caldereta f	kal·de·*re*·ta	stew
caldo m	*kal*·do	broth • consommé • stock
callos m pl	*ka*·lyos	tripe
camarón m	ka·ma·*ron*	shrimp • small prawn
canelones m pl	ka·ne·*lo*·nes	cannelloni
cangrejo m	kan·*gre*·kho	crab
— *de río*	de *ree*·o	crayfish
carabinero m	ka·ra·bee·*ne*·ro	large prawn
caracol m	ka·ra·*kol*	snail
carajillo m	ka·ra·*khee*·lyo	coffee with liqueur
carne f	*kar*·ne	meat
caza f	*ka*·tha	game (meat)
cazuela f	ka·*thwe*·la	casserole
cebolla f	the·*bo*·lya	onion
cerdo m	*ther*·do	pork
cereales m pl	the·re·*a*·les	cereal
cereza f	the·*re*·tha	cherry
champiñones m pl	cham·pee·*nyo*·nes	mushrooms
— *al ajillo*	al a·*khee*·lyo	garlic mushrooms
chanquetes m pl	chan·*ke*·tes	whitebait
charcutería f	char·koo·te·*ree*·a	cured pork meats • shop selling them
chipirón m	chee·pee·*ron*	small squid
chivo m	*chee*·vo	kid

choco m	*cho·*ko	cuttlefish
chorizo m	cho·*ree·*tho	spicy red or white sausage
— *al horno*	al *or·*no	baked spicy *chorizo*
chuleta f	choo·*le·*ta	chop · cutlet
churrasco m	choo·*ras·*ko	grilled meat or ribs in a tangy sauce · Galician meat dish
churro m	*choo·*ro	long, deep-fried doughnut
churros m pl *con chocolate*	*choo·*ros kon cho·ko·*la·*te	fried pastry strips for dunking in hot chocolate
ciruela f	theer·*we·*la	plum
cochinillo m	ko·chee·*nee·*lyo	suckling pig
cocido m	ko·*thee·*do	cooked · stew made with chickpeas, pork & chorizo
cocina f	ko·*thee·*na	kitchen
coco m	*ko·*ko	coconut
col m	kol	cabbage
coles m pl *de bruselas*	*ko·*les de broo·*se·*las	Brussels sprouts
coliflor f	ko·lee·*flor*	cauliflower
conejo m	ko·*ne·*kho	rabbit
cordero m	kor·*de·*ro	lamb
costillas f pl	kos·*tee·*lyas	ribs
croquetas f pl	kro·*ke·*tas	fried croquettes, often filled with ham or chicken
crudo/a m/f	kroo·do/a	raw
cuajada f	kwa·*kha·*da	milk junket with honey
doble m	*do·*ble	long black coffee
dorada f	do·*ra·*da	sea bass
dulce	*dool·*the	sweet
empanada f	em·pa·*na·*da	pie
ensaimada f	en·sai·*ma·*da	sweet bread (made of lard)
ensalada f	en·sa·*la·*da	salad
ensaladilla f	en·sa·la·*dee·*lya	vegetable salad
— *rusa*	*roo·*sa	vegetable salad with mayonnaise

entremeses m	en·tre·*me*·ses	hors d'oeuvres
escabeche m	es·ka·*be*·che	pickled or marinated fish
espárragos m pl	es·*pa*·ra·gos	asparagus
espagueti m	es·pa·*ge*·tee	spaghetti
espinacas f pl	es·pee·*na*·kas	spinach
estofado m	es·to·*fa*·do	stew
estofado/a m/f	es·to·*fa*·do/a	braised
faba f	*fa*·ba	type of dried bean
faisán m	fai·*san*	pheasant
fideos m pl	fee·*de*·os	thin pasta noodles with sauce
filete m	fee·*le*·te	fillet
filete m *empanado*	fee·*le*·te em·pa·*na*·do	pork, cheese & ham wrapped in breadcrumbs & fried
flan m	flan	crème caramel
frambuesa f	fram·*bwe*·sa	raspberry
fresa f	*fre*·sa	strawberry
fresco/a m/f	*fres*·ko/a	fresh
frijol m	*free*·khol	dried bean
frito/a m/f	*free*·to/a	fried
fruta f	*froo*·ta	fruit
fuerte	*fwer*·te	strong
gachos m pl	*ga*·chos	type of porridge
galleta f	ga·*lye*·ta	biscuit • cookie
gambas f pl	*gam*·bas	prawns • shrimps
— *a la plancha*	a la *plan*·cha	grilled prawns • shrimps
garbanzo m	gar·*ban*·tho	chickpea
gazpacho m	gath·*pa*·cho	cold soup made with garlic, tomato & vegetables
gazpachos m pl	gath·*pa*·chos	game dish with garlic & herbs
girasol m	*khee*·ra·sol	sunflower
granada f	gra·*na*·da	pomegranate
gratinada f	gra·tee·*na*·da	au gratin
guindilla f	gween·*dee*·lya	hot chilli pepper
guisantes m pl	gee·*san*·tes	peas

güisqui m	*gwee*·skee	whisky
hígado m	*ee*·ga·do	liver
haba f	*a*·ba	broad bean
hamburguesa f	am·boor·*ge*·sa	hamburger
harina f	a·*ree*·na	flour
helado m	e·*la*·do	ice cream
hervido/a m/f	er·*vee*·do/a	boiled
hierba buena f	*yer*·ba *bwe*·na	mint
higo m	*ee*·go	fig
hongo m	*on*·go	wild mushroom
horchata f	or·*cha*·ta	almond drink
horneado/a m/f	or·ne·*a*·do/a	baked
horno m	*or*·no	oven
hortalizas f pl	or·ta·*lee*·thas	vegetables
huevo m	*we*·vo	egg
huevos m pl	*we*·vos	scrambled eggs
revueltos	re·*vwel*·tos	
infusión f	een·foo·*syon*	herbal tea
jabalí m	kha·ba·*lee*	wild boar
jamón m	kha·*mon*	ham
— dulce	*dool*·the	boiled ham
— serrano	se·*ra*·no	cured ham
jengibre m	khen·*khee*·bre	ginger
jerez m	khe·*reth*	sherry
judías f pl	khoo·*dee*·as	beans
— verdes	*ver*·des	green beans
— blancas	*blan*·kas	butter beans
langosta f	lan·*gos*·ta	spiny lobster
langostino m	lan·gos·*tee*·no	large prawn
lechuga f	le·*choo*·ga	lettuce
legumbre m	le·*goom*·bre	pulse
lengua f	*len*·gwa	tongue
lenguado m	len·*gwa*·do	sole
lentejas f pl	len·*te*·khas	lentils
lima f	*lee*·ma	lime

limón m	lee-*mon*	lemon
lomo m	*lo*-mo	pork loin • sausage
lomo m	*lo*-mo	pork sausage
con pimientos	kon pee-*myen*-tos	with peppers
longaniza f	lon-ga-*nee*-tha	dark pork sausage
macarrones m pl	ma-ka-*ro*-nes	macaroni
magdalena f	mag-da-*le*-na	fairy cake
		(often dunked in coffee)
maíz f	ma-*eeth*	sweet corn
mandarina f	man-da-*ree*-na	tangerine
mango m	*man*-go	mango
manzana f	man-*tha*-na	apple
manzanilla f	man-tha-*nee*-lya	camomile • type of sherry •
		type of olive
marinado/a m/f	ma-ree-na-do/a	marinated
marisco m	ma-*rees*-ko	shellfish
martini m	mar-*tee*-nee	martini
mayonesa f	ma-yo-*ne*-sa	mayonnaise
mejillones m pl	me-khee-*lyo*-nes	mussels
— *al vapor*	al va-*por*	steamed mussels
melocotón m	mel-ko-*ton*	peach
melón m	me-*lon*	melon
membrillo m	mem-*bree*-lyo	quince
menta f	*men*-ta	mint
menú m *del día*	me-*noo* del *dee*-a	set menu
merluza f	mer-*loo*-tha	hake
— *a la plancha*	a la *plan*-cha	fried hake
miel f	myel	honey
migas f pl	*mee*-gas	fried breadcrumb dish
mojama f	mo-*kha*-ma	cured tuna
montado m	mon-*ta*-do	tiny tapas sandwich
morcilla f	mor-*thee*-lya	blood sausage
muy hecho	mooy e-cho	well done
naranja f	na-*ran*-kha	orange
nata f	*na*-ta	cream

39

natillas f pl	na·*tee*·lyas	creamy milk dessert
nuez f	nweth	nut • walnut
orejón m	o·re·*khon*	dried apricot
ostras f pl	*os*·tras	oysters
paella f	pa·e·lya	rice & seafood dish (some varieties contain meat)
paloma f	pa·*lo*·ma	pigeon
pan m	pan	bread
parrilla f	pa·*ree*·lya	grilled
pasa f	*pa*·sa	raisin
pastas f pl	*pa*·stas	small cakes (available in a variety of flavours)
pastel m	pas·*tel*	cake • pastry
patatas f pl	pa·*ta*·tas	potatoes
— *alioli*	a·*lyo*·lee	garlic potatoes
— *bravas*	*bra*·vas	spicy, fried potatoes
patatas f pl *fritas*	pa·*ta*·tas *free*·tas	chips • French fries
patisería f	pa·tee·se·*ree*·a	cake shop
pato m	*pa*·to	duck
pavía f	pa·*vee*·a	battered
pavo m	*pa*·vo	turkey
pechuga f	pe·*choo*·ga	chicken breast
pepino m	pe·*pee*·no	cucumber
pera f	*pe*·ra	pear
perdiz f	per·*deeth*	partridge
peregrina f	pe·re·*gree*·na	scallop
pescadilla f	pes·ka·*dee*·lya	whiting
pescado m	pes·*ka*·do	fish
pescaíto m *frito*	pes·*kai*·to *free*·to	tiny fried fish
pez espada f	peth es·*pa*·da	swordfish
picadillo m	pee·ka·*dee*·lyo	minced meat
picante	pee·*kan*·te	spicy
pil pil m	peel peel	garlic sauce (sometimes with chilli)

pimienta f	pee·*myen*·ta	pepper
pimiento m	pee·*myen*·to	capsicum • pepper
pinchitos m pl	peen·*chee*·tos	Moroccan-style kebabs
pincho m	*peen*·cho	small tapas serving
piña f	*pee*·nya	pineapple
piñón m	pee·*nyon*	pine nut
pistacho m	pees·*ta*·cho	pistachio
plancha f	*plan*·cha	grill
plátano m	*pla*·ta·no	banana
platija f	pla·*tee*·kha	flounder
plato m	*pla*·to	plate
poco hecho	po·ko e·cho	rare
pollo m	*po*·lyo	chicken
postre m	*pos*·tre	dessert
potaje m	po·*ta*·khe	stew
primer plato m	pree·*mer pla*·to	entrée • first course
puerro m	*pwe*·ro	leek
pulpo m	*pool*·po	octopus
— *a la gallega*	a la ga·*lye*·ga	octopus in sauce
queso m	*ke*·so	cheese
rabo m	*ra*·bo	tail
ración f	ra·*thyon*	small tapas plate or dish
rape m	*ra*·pe	monkfish
rebozado/a m/f	re·bo·*tha*·do/a	battered & fried
refrescos m pl	re·*fres*·kos	soft drinks
relleno/a m/f	re·*lye*·no/a	stuffed
remolacha f	re·mo·*la*·cha	beet
riñón m	ree·*nyon*	kidney
ron m	ron	rum
rosada f	ro·*sa*·da	ocean catfish • wolffish
sal f	sal	salt
salado/a m/f	sa·*la*·do/a	salted • salty
salchicha f	sal·*chee*·cha	fresh pork sausage
salchichón f	sal·chee·*chon*	peppery white sausage
salmón f	sal·*mon*	salmon

sandía f	san·*dee*·a	watermelon
sangría f	san·*gree*·a	*sangria* (red wine punch)
sardina f	sar·*dee*·na	sardine
seco/a m/f	*se*·ko/a	dry • dried
segundo plato m	se·*goon*·do *pla*·to	main course
sepia f	*se*·pya	cuttlefish
serrano m	se·*ra*·no	mountain-cured ham
sesos m pl	*se*·sos	brains
seta f	*se*·ta	wild mushroom
sidra f	*see*·dra	cider
sobrasada f	so·bra·*sa*·da	soft pork sausage
soja f	*so*·kha	soy
solomillo m	so·lo·*mee*·lyo	sirloin
sopa f	*so*·pa	soup
tapas f pl	*ta*·pas	bite-sized snacks
tarta f	*tar*·ta	cake
té m	te	tea
ternera f	ter·*ne*·ra	beef • veal
tinto	*teen*·to	red
tocino m	to·*thee*·no	bacon
tomate m	to·*ma*·te	tomato
torta f	*tor*·ta	round flat bun • cake
tortilla f	tor·*tee*·lya	omelette
— *de patata*	de pa·*ta*·ta	egg & potato omelette
— *española*	es·pa·*nyo*·la	potato omelette
tostada f	tos·*ta*·da	toast
trigo m	*tree*·go	wheat
trucha f	*troo*·cha	trout
trufa f	*troo*·fa	truffle
turrón m	too·*ron*	almond nougat
uva f	*oo*·va	grape
vaca f *(carne de)*	*va*·ka (*kar*·ne de)	beef
vegetal m	ve·khe·*tal*	vegetable
venera f	ve·*ne*·ra	scallop
verdura f	ver·*doo*·ra	green vegetable

42

vieira f	vyey·ra	scallop
vino m	vee·no	wine
— *de la casa*	de la ka·sa	house wine
zanahoria f	tha·na·o·rya	carrot
zarzuela f	thar·thwe·la	fish stew
zarzuela f *de marisco*	thar·thwe·la de ma·rees·ko	shellfish stew

Top tapas

Tapas are scrumptious cooked bar snacks, available pretty much around the clock at bars and some clubs. Take your pick from among these commonly found tasty morsels:

anchoas fritas a la catalana   an·cho·as free·tas a la ka·ta·la·na
deep-fried anchovies

bacalao   ba·ka·low
cod – usually salted and dried – prepared in various ways

boquerones   bo·ke·ro·nes
fresh anchovies marinated in wine vinegar

callos   ka·lyos
tripe – a popular Madrid tapa

caracoles   ka·ra·ko·les
snails – sometimes served *a la riojana* (in a paprika sauce)

gambas al ajillo   gam·bas al a·khee·lyo
garlic prawns • garlic shrimps

garbanzos con espinacas   gar·ban·thos kon es·pee·na·kas
chickpeas with spinach

pulpo gallego   pool·po ga·lye·go
boiled octopus in a spicy sauce

tortilla española   tor·tee·lya es·pa·nyo·la
potato and onion omelette

43

SERVICES
Post office

I want to send a ...	*Quisiera enviar ...*	kee·*sye*·ra en·vee·*ar* ...
fax	*un fax*	oon faks
parcel	*un paquete*	oon pa·*ke*·te
postcard	*una postal*	*oo*·na pos·*tal*
I want to buy (an) ...	*Quisiera comprar ...*	kee·*sye*·ra kom·*prar* ...
envelope	*un sobre*	oon *so*·bre
some stamps	*sellos*	se·lyos
Please send it	*Por favor, mándelo*	por fa·*vor* man·de·lo
(to Australia) by ...	*(a Australia) por ...*	(a ows·*tra*·lya) por ...
airmail	*vía aérea*	vee·a a·e·re·a
express post	*correo urgente*	ko·*re*·o oor·*khen*·te
registered mail	*correo*	ko·*re*·o
	certificado	ther·tee·fee·*ka*·do
surface mail	*vía terrestre*	vee·a te·*res*·tre

Bank

Where can I ...?	*¿Dónde puedo ...?*	*don*·de *pwe*·do ...
I'd like to ...	*Me gustaría ...*	me goos·ta·*ree*·a ...
cash a cheque	*cambiar un cheque*	kam·*byar* oon *che*·ke
change a	*cobrar un*	ko·*brar* oon
travellers	*cheque de*	*che*·ke de
cheque	*viajero*	vee·a·*khe*·ro
change money	*cambiar dinero*	kam·*byar* dee·*ne*·ro
get a cash	*obtener un*	ob·te·*ner* oon
advance	*adelanto*	a·de·*lan*·to
withdraw money	*sacar dinero*	sa·*kar* dee·*ne*·ro

What time does the bank open?
¿A qué hora abre el banco?   a ke *o*·ra *a*·bre el *ban*·ko

Can I arrange a transfer?
¿Puedo hacer una   *pwe*·do a·*ther oo*·na
transferencia?   trans·fe·*ren*·thya

Where's the nearest foreign exchange office?
¿Dónde está la oficina de   *don*·de es·*ta* la o·fee·*thee*·na de
cambio más cercano?   *kam*·byo mas ther·*ka*·no

Where's the nearest ATM?
¿Dónde está el cajero   *don*·de es·*ta* el ka·*khe*·ro
automatico más cercano?   ow·to·*ma*·tee·ko o mas ther·*ka*·no

What's the ...?	*¿Cuál es ...?*	kwal es ...
exchange rate	*el tipo de cambio*	el *tee*·po de *kam*·byo
commission	*la comisión?*	la ko·mee·*syon*

Phone

What's your phone number?
¿Cuál es su/tu número   kwal es soo/too *noo*·me·ro
de teléfono? pol/inf   de te·*le*·fo·no

Where's the nearest public phone?
¿Dónde hay una   *don*·de ai *oo*·na
cabina telefónica?   ka·*bee*·na te·le·*fo*·nee·ka

I want to buy a phone card.
Quiero comprar una   *kye*·ro kom·*prar oo*·na
tarjeta telefónica.   tar·*khe*·ta te·le·*fo*·nee·ka

I want to make a	*Quiero hacer ...*	*kye*·ro a·*ther ...*
... (to Singapore).	*(a Singapur).*	(a seen·ga·*poor*)
call	*una llamada*	*oo*·na lya·*ma*·da
reverse-charge/	*una llamada a*	*oo*·na lya·*ma*·da a
collect call	*cobro revertido*	*ko*·bro re·ver·*tee*·do

How much does ... cost?	¿Cuánto cuesta ...?	kwan·to kwes·ta ...
a (three)-minute call	una llamada de (tres) minutos	oo·na lya·ma·da de (tres) mee·noo·tos
each extra minute	cada minuto extra	ka·da mee·noo·to ek·stra

I want to speak for (three) minutes.
Quiero hablar por (tres) minutos.
kye·ro a·blar por (tres) mee·noo·tos

The number is ...
El número es ...
el noo·me·ro es ...

Mobile/cell phone

What are the rates?
¿Cuál es la tarifa?   kwal es la ta·ree·fa

(30c) per (30) seconds.
(Treinta centavos) por (treinta) segundos.
(treyn·ta then·ta·vos) por (treyn·ta) se·goon·dos

I'd like a/an ...	Quisiera ...	kee·sye·ra ...
adaptor plug	un adaptador	oon a·dap·ta·dor
charger for my phone	un cargador para mi teléfono	oon kar·ga·dor pa·ra mee te·le·fo·no
mobile/cell phone for hire	un móvil para alquilar	oon mo·veel pa·ra al·kee·lar
prepaid phone card	una tarjeta prepagada	oo·na tar·khe·ta pre·pa·ga·da
SIM card for your network	una tarjeta SIM para su red	oo·na tar·khe·ta seem pa·ra soo red

Internet

Where's the local internet cafe?
¿Dónde hay un   *don*·de ai oon
cibercafé cercano?   thee·ber·ka·fe ther·ka·no

How much per hour?
¿Cuánto cuesta por hora?   kwan·to kwes·ta por o·ra

How much per page?
¿Cuánto cuesta por página?   kwan·to kwes·ta por pa·khee·na

How much per CD?
¿Cuánto cuesta por cómpact?   kwan·to kwes·ta por kom·pakt

How do I log on?
¿Cómo entro al sistema?   ko·mo en·tro al sees·te·ma

It's crashed.
Se ha quedado colgado.   se a ke·da·do kol·ga·do

I've finished.
He terminado.   e ter·mee·na·do

I'd like to ...	*Quisiera ...*	kee·sye·ra ...
check my email	*revisar mi correo electrónico*	re·vee·sar mee ko·re·o e·lek·tro·nee·ko
get internet access	*usar el internet*	oo·sar el een·ter·net
use a printer	*usar una impresora*	oo·sar oo·na eem·pre·so·ra
use a scanner	*usar un escáner*	oo·sar oon es·ka·ner

Do you have ...?	*¿Tiene ...?*	tye·ne ...
Macs	*Apples*	a·pels
PCs	*PCs*	pe thes
a Zip drive	*unidad de Zip*	oo·nee·da de theep

47

GO
Directions

Where's (the Plaza Mayor)?
¿Dónde está (La Plaza Mayor)?   *don·*de es·*ta* (la *pla·*tha ma·*yor)*

I'm looking for (La Rambla).
Busco (La Rambla).   *boos·*ko (la *ram·*bla)

Which way is …?
¿Por dónde se va a …?   por *don·*de se va a …

How far is it?
¿A cuánta distancia está?   a *kwan·*ta dees·*tan·*thya es·*ta*

What's the address?
¿Cuál es la dirección?   kwal es la dee·rek·*thyon*

Can you show me (on the map)?
¿Me lo puede indicar   me lo *pwe·*de een·dee·*kar*
(en el mapa)?   (en el *ma·*pa)

It's …	*Está …*	es·*ta …*
behind …	*detrás de …*	de·*tras* de …
beside …	*al lado de …*	al *la·*do de …
far away	*lejos*	*le·*khos
here	*aquí*	a·*kee*
in front of …	*enfrente de …*	en·*fren·*te de …
left	*por la izquierda*	por la eeth·*kyer·*da
near	*cerca*	*ther·*ka
next to …	*al lado de …*	al *la·*do de …
on the corner	*en la esquina*	en la es·*kee·*na
opposite …	*frente a …*	*fren·*te a …
right	*por la derecha*	por la de·*re·*cha
straight ahead	*todo recto*	*to·*do *rek·*to
there	*ahí*	a·*ee*

It's ...	Está ...	es·ta ...
... kilometres	... kilómetros	... kee·lo·me·tros
... metres	... metros	... me·tros
... minutes	... minutos	... mee·noo·tos

Turn ...	Doble ...	do·ble ...
at the corner	en la esquina	en la es·kee·na
at the traffic lights	en el semáforo	en el se·ma·fo·ro
left/right	a la izquierda/ derecha	a la eeth·kyer·da/ de·re·cha

by bus	por autobús	por ow·to·boos
by metro	en metro	en me·tro
by taxi	por taxi	por tak·see
by train	por tren	por tren
on foot	a pie	a pye

north	nor m	nor
south	sur m	soor
east	este m	es·te
west	oeste m	wes·te

Getting around

What time does the ... leave?	¿A qué hora sale el ...?	a ke o·ra sa·le el ...
boat	barco	bar·ko
bus (city)	autobús	ow·to·boos
bus (intercity)	autocar	ow·to·kar
plane	avión	a·vyon
train	tren	tren
tram	tranvía	tran·vee·a

What time's the ... (bus)?	¿A qué hora es el ... (autobús)?	a ke *o*·ra es el ... (ow·to·*boos*)
first	primer	pree·*mer*
last	último	*ool*·tee·mo
next	próximo	*prok*·see·mo

I want to get off ...	Quiero bajarme ...	*kye*·ro ba·*khar*·me ...
at (Seville)	en (Sevilla)	en (se·*vee*·lya)
here	aquí	a·*kee*

How many stops to ...?
¿Cuántas paradas hay hasta ...?
kwan·tas pa·*ra*·das ai *as*·ta ...

Can you tell me when we get to ...?
¿Me podría decir cuándo lleguemos a ...?
me po·*dree*·a de·*theer kwan*·do lye·*ge*·mos a ...

Is this seat free?
¿Está libre este asiento?
es·*ta lee*·bre *es*·te a·*syen*·to

That's my seat.
Ése es mi asiento.
e·se es mee a·*syen*·to

Tickets & luggage

Where can I buy a ticket?
¿Dónde puedo comprar un billete?
don·de *pwe*·do kom·*prar* oon bee·*lye*·te

Do I need to book?
¿Tengo que reservar?
ten·go ke re·ser·*var*

How long does the trip take?
¿Cuánto se tarda?
kwan·to se *tar*·da

A one-way ticket to (Cádiz).
Un billete sencillo a (Cádiz).
oon bee·*lye*·te sen·*thee*·lyo a (*ka*·deeth)

I'd like to ...	Me gustaría ...	me goos·ta·*ree*·a ...
my ticket.	mi billete.	mee bee·*lye*·te
cancel	cancelar	kan·the·*lar*
change	cambiar	kam·*byar*
confirm	confirmar	kon·feer·*mar*

One ... ticket,	Un billete ...,	oon bee·*lye*·te ...
please.	por favor.	por fa·*vor*
1st-class	de primera clase	de pree·*me*·ra *kla*·se
2nd-class	de segunda clase	de se·*goon*·da *kla*·se
child's	infantil	een·fan·*teel*
return	de ida y vuelta	de *ee*·da ee *vwel*·ta
student's	de estudiante	de es·too·*dyan*·te

I'd like a/an	Quisiera un	kee·*sye*·ra oon
... seat.	asiento ...	a·*syen*·to ...
aisle	de pasillo	de pa·*see*·lyo
nonsmoking	de no fumadores	de no foo·ma·*do*·res
smoking	de fumadores	de foo·ma·*do*·res
window	junto a la ventana	*khoon*·to a la ven·*ta*·na

Is there (a) ...?	¿Hay ...?	ai ...
air-conditioning	aire	*ai*·re
	acondicionado	a·kon·dee·thyo·*na*·do
blanket	una manta	*oo*·na *man*·ta
toilet	servicios	ser·*vee*·thyos
video	vídeo	*vee*·de·o

Is it a direct route?
  ¿Es un viaje directo?   es oon *vya*·khe dee·*rek*·to

What time do I have to check in?
  ¿A qué hora tengo que   a ke *o*·ra *ten*·go ke
  facturar mi equipaje?   fak·too·*rar* mee e·kee·*pa*·khe

Can I get a stand-by ticket?

*¿Puede ponerme en
la lista de espera?*

pwe·de po·*ner*·me en
la *lees*·ta de es·*pe*·ra

I'd like a luggage locker.

*Quisiera un casillero
de consigna.*

kee·*sye*·ra oon ka·see·*lye*·ro
de kon·*seeg*·na

Can I have some coins/tokens?

*¿Me podría dar
monedas/fichas?*

me po·*dree*·a dar
mo·*ne*·das/*fee*·chas

Where's the baggage claim?

*¿Dónde está la recogida de
equipages?*

don·de es·*ta* la re·ko·*khee*·da de
e·kee·*pa*·khes

My luggage	Mis maletas	mees ma·*le*·tas
has been ...	han sido ...	an *see*·do ...
damaged	dañadas	da·*nya*·das
lost	perdidas	per·*dee*·das
stolen	robadas	ro·*ba*·das

Bus, metro, taxi & train

Which city/intercity bus goes to ...?

¿Qué autobús/autocar va a ...? ke ow·to·*boos*/ow·to·*kar* va a ...

Is this the bus to ...?

¿Es el autobús para ...? es el ow·to·*boos* pa·ra ...

What station is this?

¿Cuál es esta estación? kwal es *es*·ta es·ta·*thyon*

What's the next station?

¿Cuál es la próxima estación? kwal es la *prok*·see·ma es·ta·*thyon*

Does this train stop at (Aranjuez)?
¿Para el tren en (Aranjuez)?   pa·ra el tren en (a·*ran*·khweth)

Do I need to change trains?
¿Tengo que cambiar de tren?   *ten*·go ke kam·*byar* de tren

How many stops to (the museum)?
¿Cuántas paradas hay   *kwan*·tas pa·*ra*·das ai
hasta (el museo)?   *as*·ta (el moo·*se*·o)

Which carriage is ...?	*¿Cuál es el coche ...?*	kwal es el *ko*·che ...
for (Valencia)	*para (Valencia)*	*pa*·ra (va·*len*·thya)
1st class	*de primera clase*	de pree·*me*·ra *kla*·se
for dining	*comedor*	ko·me·*dor*

I'd like a taxi ...	*Quisiera un taxi ...*	kee·*sye*·ra oon *tak*·see ...
at (9am)	*a (las nueve de la mañana)*	a (las *nwe*·ve de la ma·*nya*·na)
now	*ahora*	a·*o*·ra
tomorrow	*mañana*	ma·*nya*·na

Is this taxi free?
¿Está libre este taxi?   es·ta *lee*·bre *es*·te *tak*·see

Please put the meter on.
Por favor, ponga el   por fa·*vor* pon·ga el
taxímetro.   tak·*see*·me·tro

How much is it to ...?
¿Cuánto cuesta ir a ...?   *kwan*·to *kwes*·ta eer a ...

Please take me to (this address).
Por favor, lléveme   por fa·*vor* lye·ve·me
a (esta dirección).   a (*es*·ta dee·rek·*thyon*)

Please ...	Por favor ...	por fa·*vor* ...
slow down	*vaya más despacio*	*va*·ya mas des·*pa*·thyo
wait here	*espere aquí*	es·*pe*·re a·*kee*

Stop ...	Pare ...	*pa*·re ...
at the corner	*en la esquina*	en la es·*kee*·na
here	*aquí*	a·*kee*

Car & motorbike hire

I'd like to hire	Quisiera	kee·*sye*·ra
a/an ...	*alquilar* ...	al·*kee*·lar ...
(small/large) car	*un coche (grande/ pequeño)*	oon *ko*·che (*gran*·de/ pe·*ke*·nyo)
motorbike	*una moto*	*oo*·na *mo*·to

with ...	con ...	kon ...
air-conditioning	*aire acondicionado*	*ai*·re a·kon·dee·thyo·*na*·do
antifreeze	*anticongelante*	an·tee·kon·khe·*lan*·te
snow chains	*cadenas de nieve*	ka·*de*·nas de *nye*·ve

How much for ... hire?	¿Cuánto cuesta el alquiler por ...?	*kwan*·to *kwes*·ta el al·*kee*·ler por ...
daily	*día*	*dee*·a
hourly	*hora*	*o*·ra
weekly	*semana*	se·*ma*·na

Does that include insurance/mileage?

¿Incluye el seguro/ kilometraje?	een·*kloo*·ye el se·*goo*·ro/ kee·lo·me·*tra*·khe

54

Is this the road to ...?
¿Se va a ... por esta carretera?
se va a ... por *es*·ta ka·re·*te*·ra

Where's a petrol station?
¿Dónde hay una gasolinera?
don·de ai *oo*·na ga·so·lee·*ne*·ra

(How long) Can I park here?
¿(Por cuánto tiempo) Puedo aparcar aquí?
(por *kwan*·to tyem·po) *pwe*·do a·par·*kar* a·*kee*

What's the ...
speed limit?
city
country

¿Cuál es el límite de velocidad ...?
en la ciudad
en el campo

kwal es el *lee*·mee·te de ve·lo·thee·*da* ...
en la theew·*da*
en el *kam*·po

Road signs

Acceso	ak·*the*·so	Entrance
Aparcamiento	a·par·ka·*myen*·to	Parking
Ceda el Paso	*the*·da el *pa*·so	Give Way
Desvío	des·*vee*·o	Detour
Dirección Única	dee·rek·*thyon oo*·nee·ka	One Way
Frene	*fre*·ne	Slow Down
Peaje	pe·*a*·khe	Toll
Peligro	pe·*lee*·gro	Danger
Prohibido Aparcar	pro·ee·*bee*·do a·par·*kar*	No Parking
Prohibido el Paso	pro·ee·*bee*·do el *pa*·so	No Entry
Stop	es·*top*	Stop
Vía de Acceso	*vee*·a de ak·*the*·so	Freeway Entrance

SLEEP
Finding accommodation

Where's a ...?	¿Dónde hay ...?	don·de ai ...
bed and breakfast	una pensión con desayuno	oo·na pen·syon kon de·sa·yoo·no
camping ground	terreno de cámping	te·re·no de kam·peen
guest house	una pensión	oo·na pen·syon
hotel	un hotel	oon o·tel
youth hostel	un albergue juvenil	oon al·ber·ge khoo·ve·neel

Can you recommend somewhere ...?	¿Puede recomendar algún sitio ...?	pwe·de re·ko·men·dar al·goon see·tee·o ...
cheap	barato	ba·ra·to
luxurious	de lujo	de loo·kho
nearby	cercano	ther·ka·no
nice	agradable	a·gra·da·ble
romantic	romántico	ro·man·tee·ko

What's the address?
¿Cuál es la dirección?   kwal es la dee·rek·thyon

Booking ahead & checking in

I'd like to book a room, please.
Quisiera reservar   kee·sye·ra re·ser·var
una habitación.   oo·na a·bee·ta·thyon

I have a reservation.
He hecho una reserva.   e e·cho oo·na re·ser·va

My name's ...
Me llamo ...   me lya·mo ...

Do you have a ... room?	¿Tiene una habitación ...?	tye·ne oo·na a·bee·ta·thyon ...
double	doble	do·ble
single	individual	een·dee·vee·dwal
twin	con dos camas	kon dos ka·mas

How much is it per ...?	¿Cuánto cuesta por ...?	kwan·to kwes·ta por ...
night	noche	no·che
person	persona	per·so·na
week	semana	se·ma·na

For (three) nights.
Por (tres) noches.   por (tres) no·ches

From (July 2) to (July 6).
Desde (el dos de julio)   des·de (el dos de khoo·lyo)
hasta (el seis de julio).   as·ta (el seys de khoo·lyo)

Can I see it?
¿Puedo verla?   pwe·do ver·la

It's fine. I'll take it.
Vale, la alquilo.   va·le la al·kee·lo

Do I need to pay upfront?
¿Necesito pagar por   ne·the·see·to pa·gar por
adelantado?   a·de·lan·ta·do

Do you accept ...?	¿Aceptan ...?	a·thep·tan ...
credit cards	tarjetas de crédito	tar·khe·tas de kre·dee·to
debit cards	tarjetas de débito	tar·khe·tas de de·bee·to
travellers cheques	cheques de viajero	che·kes de vya·khe·ro

Requests & queries

When/Where is breakfast served?
*¿Cuándo/Dónde se sirve
el desayuno?*
kwan·do/don·de se seer·ve
el de·sa·yoo·no

Please wake me at (seven).
*Por favor, despiérteme
a (las siete).*
por fa·vor des·pyer·te·me
a (las sye·te)

Can I use the ...?	*¿Puedo usar ...?*	pwe·do oo·sar ...
kitchen	*la cocina*	la ko·thee·na
laundry	*el lavadero*	el la·va·de·ro
telephone	*el teléfono*	el te·le·fo·no
Is there a/an ...?	*¿Hay ...?*	ai ...
elevator	*ascensor*	as·then·sor
laundry service	*servicio de
lavandería*	ser·vee·thyo de
la·van·de·ree·a
safe	*una caja fuerte*	oo·na ka·kha fwer·te
Do you ... here?	*¿Aquí ...?*	a·kee ...
arrange tours	*organizan
recorridos*	or·ga·nee·than
re·ko·ree·dos
change money	*cambian dinero*	kam·byan dee·ne·ro
It's too ...	*Es demasiado ...*	es de·ma·sya·do ...
cold	*fría*	free·a
dark	*oscura*	os·koo·ra
expensive	*cara*	ka·ra
light	*clara*	kla·ra
noisy	*ruidosa*	rwee·do·sa
small	*pequeña*	pe·ke·nya

The ... doesn't work.	No funciona ...	no foon·*thyo*·na ...
air-conditioning	el aire	el *ai*·re
	acondicionado	a·kon·dee·thyo·*na*·do
fan	el ventilador	el ven·tee·la·*dor*
toilet	el retrete	el re·*tre*·te
window	la ventana	la ven·*ta*·na

Can I get	¿Puede darme	*pwe*·de *dar*·me
another ...?	otra ...?	*o*·tra ...
This ... isn't clean.	Ésta ... no está limpia.	es·ta ... no es·*ta leem*·pya
blanket	manta	*man*·ta
pillow	almohada	al·*mwa*·da
pillowcase	funda de almohada	*foon*·da de al·*mwa*·da
sheet	sábana	*sa*·ba·na
towel	toalla	*twa*·lya

Checking out

What time is check out?
¿A qué hora hay que dejar   a ke *o*·ra ai ke de·*khar*
libre la habitación?   *lee*·bre la a·bee·ta·*thyon*

Can I leave my bags here?
¿Puedo dejar las maletas aquí?   *pwe*·do de·*khar* las ma·*le*·tas a·*kee*

Could I have ...,	¿Me puede dar ...,	me *pwe*·de dar ...
please?	por favor?	por fa·*vor*
my deposit	mi depósito	mee de·*po*·see·to
my passport	mi pasaporte	mee pa·sa·*por*·te
my valuables	mis objetos	mees ob·*khe*·tos
	de valor	de va·*lor*

I'll be back ...	Volveré ...	vol·ve·*re* ...
in (three) days	en (tres) días	en (tres) *dee*·as
on (Tuesday)	el (martes)	el (*mar*·tes)

WORK
Introductions

Where's the ...?	¿Dónde está ...?	don·de es·ta ...
business centre	el servicio	el ser·vee·thyo
	secretarial	se·kre·ta·ryal
conference	el congreso	el kon·gre·so

I'm attending a ...	Asisto a ...	a·sees·to a ...
conference	un congreso	oon kon·gre·so
course	un curso	oon koor·so
meeting	una reunión	oo·na re·oo·nyon
trade fair	una feria de	oo·na fe·rya de
	muestras	mwes·tras

I'm with ...	Estoy con ...	es·toy kon ...
(the UN)	(el ONU)	(el o en oo)
my colleague(s)	mi(s) colega(s)	mee(s) ko·le·ga(s)
(two) others	otros (dos)	ot·ros (dos)

Here's my business card.
Aquí tiene mi tarjeta de visita.
a·kee tye·ne mee tar·khe·ta de vee·see·ta

Let me introduce my colleague.
¿Puedo presentarle a mi compañero/a? m/f
pwe·do pre·sen·tar·le a mee kom·pa·nye·ro/a

I'm alone.
Estoy solo/a. m/f
es·toy so·lo/a

I'm staying at ..., room ...
Me estoy alojando en ..., la habitación ...
me es·toy a·lo·khan·do en ..., la a·bee·ta·thyon ...

I'm here for (two) days/weeks.
Estoy aquí por (dos) días/semanas.
es·toy a·kee por (dos) dee·as/se·ma·nas

Business needs

I have an appointment with …
Tengo una cita con …   *ten·*go *oo·*na *thee·*ta kon …

I'm expecting …	*Estoy esperando …*	es·*toy* es·pe·*ran·*do …
a call	*una llamada*	*oo·*na lya·*ma·*da
a fax	*un fax*	oon faks
I need …	*Necesito …*	ne·se·*thee·*to …
a connection to	*una conexión*	*oo·*na ko·nek·*syon*
the Net	*al internet*	al een·ter·*net*
an interpreter	*un/una*	oon/*oo·*na
	intérprete m&f	een·*ter·*pre·te
to make	*hacer*	a·*ther*
photocopies	*fotocopias*	fo·to·*ko·*pyas
to send an	*enviar un*	en·*vyar* oon
email/fax	*email/fax*	*ee·*mayl/faks
laser pointer	*puntero* m *láser*	poon·*te·*ro *la·*ser
overhead	*retroproyector* m	re·tro·pro·yek·*tor*
projector	*de transparencias*	de tran·spa·*ren·*thyas
whiteboard	*pizarra* f *blanca*	pee·*tha·*ra *blan·*ka

After the deal

That went very well.
Eso fue muy bien.   *e·*so fwe mooy byen

Shall we go for a drink/meal?
¿Vamos a tomar/   *va·*mos a to·*mar/*
comer algo?   ko·*mer* al·go

It's on me.
Invito yo.   een·*vee·*to yo

HELP
Emergencies

Help!	*¡Socorro!*	so·*ko*·ro
Stop!	*¡Pare!*	*pa*·re
Go away!	*¡Váyase!*	*va*·ya·se
Thief!	*¡Ladrón!*	lad·*ron*
Fire!	*¡Fuego!*	*fwe*·go
Watch out!	*¡Cuidado!*	kwee·*da*·do

It's an emergency.
Es una emergencia. es *oo*·na e·mer·*khen*·thya

Call the police!
¡Llame a la policía! *lya*·me a la po·lee·*thee*·a

Call a doctor!
¡Llame a un médico! *lya*·me a oon *me*·dee·ko

Call an ambulance!
¡Llame a una ambulancia! *lya*·me a *oo*·na am·boo·*lan*·thya

Could you help me, please?
¿Me puede ayudar, por favor? me *pwe*·de a·yoo·*dar* por fa·*vor*

I have to use the telephone.
Necesito usar el teléfono. ne·the·*see*·to oo·*sar* el te·*le*·fo·no

I'm lost.
Estoy perdido/a. m/f es·*toy* per·*dee*·do/a

Where are the toilets?
¿Dónde están los servicios? *don*·de es·*tan* los ser·*vee*·thyos

Leave me alone!
¡Déjame en paz! de·*kha*·me en path

Police

Where's the police station?
¿Dónde está la comisaría? · don·de es·ta la ko·mee·sa·ree·a

I want to report an offence.
Quiero denunciar un delito. · kye·ro de·noon·thyar oon de·lee·to

I've been assaulted.
He sido asaltado/a. m/f · e see·do a·sal·ta·do/a

I've been robbed.
Me han robado. · me an ro·ba·do

I've been raped.
He sido violado/a. m/f · e see·do vee·o·la·do/a

My ... was stolen.
Mi ... fue robado/a. m/f · mee ... fwe ro·ba·do/a

My ... were stolen.
Mis ... fueron robados/as. m/f · mees ... fwe·ron ro·ba·dos/as

I've lost my ...	*He perdido ...*	e per·dee·do ...
backpack	*mi mochila*	mee mo·chee·la
bags	*mis maletas*	mees ma·le·tas
credit card	*mi tarjeta de crédito*	mee tar·khe·ta de kre·dee·to
handbag	*mi bolso*	mee bol·so
money	*mi dinero*	mee dee·ne·ro
passport	*mi pasaporte*	mee pa·sa·por·te
wallet	*mi cartera*	mee kar·te·ra

I want to contact my embassy/consulate.
Quiero ponerme en contacto con mi embajada/consulado. · kye·ro po·ner·me en kon·tak·to kon mee em·ba·kha·da/kon·soo·la·do

I have a prescription for this drug.
Tengo receta para esta droga. · ten·go re·the·ta pa·ra es·ta dro·ga

Health

Where's the	¿Dónde está . . .	don·de es·ta . . .
nearest . . .?	más cercano/a? m/f	mas ther·ka·no/a
chemist	la farmacia f	la far·ma·thya
dentist	el dentista m	el den·tees·ta
doctor	el médico m	el me·dee·ko
hospital	el hospital m	el os·pee·tal
medical centre	el consultorio m	el kon·sool·to·ryo
optometrist	el oculista m	el o·koo·lees·ta

I need a doctor (who speaks English).

Necesito un médico   ne·the·see·to oon me·dee·ko
(que hable inglés).   (ke a·ble een·gles)

Could I see a female doctor?

¿Puede examinarme   pwe·de ek·sa·mee·nar·me
una médica?   oo·na me·dee·ka

Can the doctor come here?

¿Puede visitarme el médico?   pwe·de vee·see·tar·me el me·dee·ko

I've run out of my medication.

Se me terminaron los   se me ter·mee·na·ron los
medicamentos.   me·dee·ka·men·tos

My prescription is . . .

Mi receta es . . .   mee re·se·ta es . . .

I've been vaccinated	Estoy vacunado/a	es·toy va·koo·na·do/a
against . . .	contra . . . m/f	kon·tra . . .
. . . fever	la fiebre . . .	la fye·bre . . .
hepatitis A/B/C	la hepatitis A/B/C	la e·pa·tee·tees a/be/the
tetanus	el tétano	el te·ta·no
typhoid	la tifus	la tee·foos

Symptoms, conditions & allergies

I'm sick.
Estoy enfermo/a. m/f   es·*toy* en·*fer*·mo/a

It hurts here.
Me duele aquí.   me *dwe*·le a·*kee*

I've been injured.
He sido herido/a. m/f   e *see*·do e·*ree*·do/a

I've been vomiting.
He estado vomitando.   e es·*ta*·do vo·mee·*tan*·do

I feel ...	*Me siento ...*	me *syen*·to ...
better	*mejor*	me·*khor*
dizzy	*mareado/a* m/f	ma·re·*a*·do
nauseous	*con nauseas*	kon *now*·se·as
shivery	*destemplado/a* m/f	des·tem·*pla*·do/a
worse	*peor*	pe·*or*

For more symptoms & conditions, see the dictionary in **LOOK UP**, page 70.

Do I need a prescription for ...?
¿Necesito receta para ...?   ne·the·*see*·to re·*the*·ta *pa*·ra ...

I have a prescription.
Tengo receta médica.   *ten*·go re·*the*·ta *me*·dee·ka

How many times a day?
¿Cuántas veces al día?   *kwan*·tas *ve*·thes al *dee*·a

I have ...
Tengo ...   *ten*·go ...

I've recently had ...
Hace poco he tenido ...   a·the *po*·ko e te·*nee*·do ...

I'm on regular medication for ...

Estoy bajo		es·*toy ba*·kho
medicación para ...		me·dee·ka·*thyon pa*·ra ...

asthma	*asma* m	*as*·ma
allergy	*alergia* f	a·ler·*khee*·a
bronchitis	*bronquitis* m	bron·*kee*·tees
cold	*resfriado* m	res·free·*a*·do
cough	*tos* f	tos
diabetes	*diabetes* m	dee·a·*be*·tes
diarrhoea	*diarrea* f	dee·a·*re*·a
fever	*fiebre* f	*fye*·bre
headache	*dolor* m *de cabeza*	do·lor de ka·*be*·tha
heart condition	*condición* f *cardíaca*	kon·dee·*thyon* kar·*dya*·ka
infection	*infección* f	een·fek·*thyon*
sprain	*torcedura* f	tor·the·*doo*·ra

I'm allergic to ...	*Soy alérgico/a ...* m/f	soy a·*ler*·khee·ko/a ...
antibiotics	*a los antibióticos*	a los an·tee·*byo*·tee·kos
anti-	*a los anti-*	a los an·tee·
inflammatories	*inflamatorios*	een·fla·ma·*to*·ryos
aspirin	*a la aspirina*	a la as·pee·*ree*·na
bees	*a las abejas*	a las a·*be*·khas
codeine	*a la codeína*	a la ko·de·*ee*·na
nuts	*a las nueces*	a las *nwe*·thes
peanuts	*a los cacahuetes*	a los ka·ka·*we*·tes
penicillin	*a la penicilina*	a la pe·nee·thee·*lee*·na
pollen	*al polen*	al *po*·len

I have a skin allergy.

Tengo una alergia en la piel.	*ten*·go *oo*·na a·*ler*·khya en la pyel

For more food-related allergies, see **EAT & DRINK**, page 32.

Numbers

0	cero	*the·ro*	18	dieciocho	dye·thee·o·cho	
1	uno	*oo·no*	19	diecinueve	dye·thee·nwe·ve	
2	dos	dos	20	veinte	veyn·te	
3	tres	tres	21	veintiuno	veyn·tee·oo·no	
4	cuatro	*kwa·tro*	22	veintidós	veyn·tee·dos	
5	cinco	*theen·ko*	30	treinta	treyn·ta	
6	seis	seys	40	cuarenta	kwa·ren·ta	
7	siete	*sye·te*	50	cincuenta	theen·kwen·ta	
8	ocho	o·cho	60	sesenta	se·sen·ta	
9	nueve	nwe·ve	70	setenta	se·ten·ta	
10	diez	dyeth	80	ochenta	o·chen·ta	
11	once	on·the	90	noventa	no·ven·ta	
12	doce	do·the	100	cien	thyen	
13	trece	tre·the	101	ciento uno	thyen·to oo·no	
14	catorce	ka·tor·the	102	ciento dos	thyen·to dos	
15	quince	keen·the	500	quinientos	kee·nyen·tos	
16	dieciséis	dye·thee·seys	1000	mil	meel	
17	diecisiete	dye·thee·sye·te	1 million	un millón ·	oon mee·lyon	

Colours

dark ...	... oscuro	... o·skoo·ro		grey	gris	grees
light ...	... claro	... kla·ro		orange	naranja	na·ran·kha
				pink	rosa	ro·sa
black	negro/a	ne·gro/a		purple	lila	lee·la
blue	azul	a·thool		red	rojo/a	ro·kho/a
brown	marrón	ma·ron		white	blanco/a	blan·ko/a
green	verde	ver·de		yellow	amarillo/a	a·ma·ree·lyo/a

Time & dates

What time is it?	¿Qué hora es?	ke o·ra es
It's (one) o'clock.	Es (la una).	es (la oo·na)
It's (ten) o'clock.	Son (las diez).	son (las dyeth)
Quarter past one.	Es la una y cuarto.	es la oo·na ee kwar·to
Twenty past one.	Es la una y veinte.	es la oo·na ee veyn·te
Half past one.	Es la una y media.	es la oo·na ee me·dya
Twenty to one.	Es la una menos veinte.	es la oo·na me·nos veyn·te
Quarter to one.	Es la una menos cuarto.	es la oo·na me·nos kwar·to
At what time?	¿A qué hora?	a ke o·ra
At ...	A ...	a ...
am	de la mañana	de la ma·nya·na
pm	de la tarde	de la tar·de
Monday	lunes	loo·nes
Tuesday	martes	mar·tes
Wednesday	miércoles	myer·ko·les
Thursday	jueves	khwe·ves
Friday	viernes	vyer·nes
Saturday	sábado	sa·ba·do
Sunday	domingo	do·meen·go
January	enero	e·ne·ro
February	febrero	fe·bre·ro
March	marzo	mar·tho
April	abril	a·breel
May	mayo	ma·yo
June	junio	khoo·nyo
July	julio	khoo·lyo
August	agosto	a·gos·to
September	septiembre	sep·tyem·bre
October	octubre	ok·too·bre
November	noviembre	no·vyem·bre
December	diciembre	dee·thyem·bre

spring	*primavera* f	pree·ma·*ve*·ra
summer	*verano* m	ve·*ra*·no
autumn	*otoño* m	o·*to*·nyo
winter	*invierno* m	een·*vyer*·no

What date?
¿Qué día?   ke *dee*·a

What date is it today?
¿Qué día es hoy?   ke *dee*·a es oy

It's (18 October).
Es (el dieciocho de octubre).   es (el dye·thee·o·cho de ok·*too*·bre)

last ...		
month	*el mes pasado*	el mes pa·*sa*·do
night	*anoche*	a·*no*·che
week	*la semana pasada*	la se·*ma*·na pa·*sa*·da
year	*el año pasado*	el *a*·nyo pa·*sa*·do

next ...	*... que viene*	... ke *vye*·ne
month	*el mes*	el mes
week	*la semana*	la se·*ma*·na
year	*el año*	el *a*·nyo

| since (May) | *desde (mayo)* | *des*·de (*ma*·yo) |

tomorrow ...	*mañana por la ...*	ma·*nya*·na por la ...
afternoon	*tarde*	*tar*·de
evening	*noche*	*no*·che
morning	*mañana*	ma·*nya*·na

yesterday ...	*ayer por la ...*	a·*yer* por la ...
afternoon	*tarde*	*tar*·de
evening	*noche*	*no*·che
morning	*mañana*	ma·*nya*·na

A English–Spanish dictionary

Nouns in this dictionary have their gender indicated by m (masculine) or f (feminine).
If it's a plural noun, you'll also see pl.
Where no gender is marked the word is either an adjective or a verb, with adjectives first.

A

aboard *a bordo* a *bor*·do
accident *accidente* m ak·thee·*den*·te
accommodation *alojamiento* m
a·lo·kha·*myen*·to
across *a través* a tra·*ves*
adaptor *adaptador* m a·dap·ta·*dor*
address *dirección* f dee·rek·*thyon*
admission price *precio* m *de entrada*
pre·thyo de en·*tra*·da
after *después de* des·*pwes* de
aftershave *bálsamo de aftershave*
bal·sa·mo de *af*·ter·sha·eev
again *otra vez* o·tra veth
air-conditioned *con aire acondicionado* kon
ai·re a·kon·dee·thyo·*na*·do
airline *aerolínea* f ay·ro·*lee*·nya
airplane *avión* m a·*vyon*
airport *aeropuerto* m ay·ro·*pwer*·to
airport tax *tasa* f *del aeropuerto* ta·sa del
ay·ro·*pwer*·to
alarm clock *despertador* m des·per·ta·*dor*
alcohol *alcohol* m al·*kol*
all *todo* to·do
allergy *alergia* f a·*ler*·khya
alone *solo/a* m/f *so*·lo/a
ambulance *ambulancia* m
am·boo·*lan*·thya
and *y* ee
ankle *tobillo* m to·*bee*·lyo
antibiotics *antibióticos* m pl
an·tee·byo·*tee*·kos
antique *antigüedad* f an·tee·gwe·*da*
antiseptic *antiséptico* m an·tee·*sep*·tee·ko
appointment *cita* f *thee*·ta
architect *arquitecto/a* m/f ar·kee·*tek*·to/a
architecture *arquitectura* f ar·kee·tek·*too*·ra
arm *brazo* m *bra*·tho
arrivals *llegadas* f pl lye·*ga*·das

arrive *llegar* lye·*gar*
art *arte* m *ar*·te
art gallery *museo* m *de arte* moo·*se*·o
de *ar*·te
artist *artista* m&f ar·*tees*·ta
ashtray *cenicero* m the·nee·*the*·ro
aspirin *aspirina* f as·pee·*ree*·na
assault *asalto* m a·*sal*·to
aunt *tía* f *tee*·a
Australia *Australia* f ow·*stra*·lya
automatic teller machine (ATM) *cajero* m
automático ka·*khe*·ro ow·to·*ma*·tee·ko

B

B&W (film) *blanco y negro* blan·ko ee
ne·gro
baby *bebé* m be·*be*
baby food *comida* f *de bebé* ko·*mee*·da
de be·*be*
babysitter *canguros* m kan·*goo*·ros
back (of body) *espalda* f es·*pal*·da
backpack *mochila* f mo·*chee*·la
bacon *tocino* m to·*thee*·no
bad *malo/a* m/f *ma*·lo/a
bag *bolso* m *bol*·so
baggage *equipaje* m e·kee·*pa*·khe
baggage allowance *límite* m *de equipaje*
lee·mee·te de e·kee·*pa*·khe
baggage claim *recogida* f *de equipajes*
re·ko·*khee*·da de e·kee·*pa*·khes
bakery *panadería* f pa·na·de·*ree*·a
band *grupo* m *groo*·po
bandage *vendaje* m ven·*da*·khe
Band-Aids *tiritas* f pl tee·*ree*·tas
bank *banco* m *ban*·ko
bank account *cuenta* f *bancaria* kwen·ta
ban·*ka*·rya
banknotes *billetes* m pl *(de banco)*
bee·*lye*·tes (de *ban*·ko)

English–Spanish dictionary **B**

LOOK UP ENG - SPA

bar (venue) *bar* m bar
bar (with music) *pub* m poob
bath *bañera* f ba·*nye*·ra
bathroom *baño* m *ba*·nyo
battery *pila* f *pee*·la
beach *playa* f *pla*·ya
beautiful *hermoso/a* m/f er·*mo*·so/a
beauty salon *salón* m de belleza sa·*lon* de be·*lye*·tha
bed *cama* f *ka*·ma
bedding *ropa* f de cama *ro*·pa de *ka*·ma
bedroom *habitación* f a·bee·ta·*thyon*
beer *cerveza* f ther·*ve*·tha
before *antes* an·tes
begin *comenzar* ko·men·*thar*
behind *detrás de* de·*tras* de
best *lo mejor* lo me·*khor*
better *mejor* me·*khor*
bicycle *bicicleta* f bee·thee·*kle*·ta
big *grande* gran·de
bill *cuenta* f *kwen*·ta
birthday *cumpleaños* m koom·ple·*a*·nyos
black *negro/a* m/f *ne*·gro/a
blanket *manta* f *man*·ta
blister *ampolla* f am·*po*·lya
blocked *atascado/a* m/f a·tas·*ka*·do/a
blood *sangre* f *san*·gre
blood group *grupo* m sanguíneo *groo*·po san·*gee*·neo
blue *azul* a·*thool*
board (ship etc) *embarcarse* em·bar·*kar*·se
boarding house *pensión* f pen·*syon*
boarding pass *tarjeta* f de embarque tar·*khe*·ta de em·*bar*·ke
book *libro* m *lee*·bro
book (make a reservation) *reservar* re·ser·*var*
booked out *lleno/a* m/f *lye*·no/a
bookshop *librería* f lee·bre·*ree*·a
boots *botas* f pl *bo*·tas
border *frontera* f fron·*te*·ra
boring *aburrido/a* m/f a·boo·*ree*·do/a
both *los/las dos* m/f pl los/las dos

bottle *botella* f bo·*te*·lya
bottle opener *abrebotellas* m a·bre·bo·*te*·lyas
bowl *bol* m bol
box *caja* f *ka*·kha
boy *chico* m *chee*·ko
boyfriend *novio* m *no*·vyo
bra *sujetador* m soo·khe·ta·*dor*
brakes *frenos* m pl *fre*·nos
bread *pan* m pan
breakfast *desayuno* m des·a·*yoo*·no
bridge *puente* m *pwen*·te
briefcase *maletín* m ma·le·*teen*
brochure *folleto* m fo·*lye*·to
broken *roto/a* m/f *ro*·to/a
brother *hermano* m er·*ma*·no
brown *marrón* ma·*ron*
buffet *buffet* m boo·*fe*
building *edificio* m e·dee·*fee*·thyo
bull *toro* m *to*·ro
bullfight *corrida* f ko·*ree*·da
bullring *plaza* f de toros *pla*·tha de *to*·ros
burn *quemadura* f ke·ma·*doo*·ra
bus (city) *autobús* m ow·to·*boos*
bus (intercity) *autocar* m ow·to·*kar*
bus station (city) *estación* f de autobuses es·ta·*thyon* de ow·to·*boo*·ses
bus station (intercity) *estación* f de autocares es·ta·*thyon* de ow·to·*ka*·res
bus stop *parada* f de autobús pa·*ra*·da de ow·to·*boos*
business *negocios* m pl ne·*go*·thyos
business class *clase* f preferente *kla*·se pre·fe·*ren*·te
business person *comerciante* m&f ko·mer·*thyan*·te
busker *artista callejero/a* m/f ar·*tees*·ta ka·lye·*khe*·ro/a
busy *ocupado/a* m/f o·koo·*pa*·do/a
but *pero* pe·ro
butcher's shop *carnicería* f kar·nee·the·*ree*·a
buttons *botones* m pl bo·*to*·nes
buy *comprar* kom·*prar*

71

C

cafe *cafe* m ka-*fe*
cake shop *pastelería* f pas-te-le-*ree*-a
calculator *calculadora* f kal-koo-la-*do*-ra
camera *cámara* f (*fotográfica*) *ka*-ma-ra
(fo-to-*gra*-fee-ka)
camera shop *tienda* f *de fotografía* tyen-da
de fo-to-gra-*fee*-a
campsite *cámping* m *kam*-peen
can *lata* f *la*-ta
can opener *abrelatas* m a-bre-*la*-tas
Canada *Canadá* f ka-na-*da*
cancel *cancelar* kan-the-*lar*
car *coche* m *ko*-che
car hire *alquiler* m *de coche* al-kee-*ler*
de *ko*-che
car owner's title *papeles* m pl *del coche*
pa-*pe*-les del *ko*-che
car registration *matrícula* f
ma-*tree*-koo-la
carpark *aparcamiento* m
a-par-ka-*myen*-to
cash *dinero* m *en efectivo* dee-*ne*-ro en
e-fek-*tee*-vo
cash (a cheque) *cambiar* (*un cheque*)
kam-*byar* (oon che-ke)
cash register *caja* f *registradora* ka-kha
re-khees-tra-*do*-ra
cashier *caja* f *ka*-kha
cassette *casete* m ka-*se*-te
castle *castillo* m kas-*tee*-lyo
cathedral *catedral* f ka-te-*dral*
Catholic *católico/a* m/f ka-*to*-lee-ko/a
CD *cómpact* m *kom*-pakt
cemetery *cementerio* m the-men-*te*-ryo
centimetre *centímetro* m then-*tee*-me-tro
centre *centro* m *then*-tro
chair *silla* f *see*-lya
champagne *champán* m cham-*pan*
change *cambio* m *kam*-byo
change *cambiar* kam-*byar*
changing rooms *vestuarios* m pl
ves-*twa*-ryos

cheap *barato/a* m/f ba-*ra*-to/a
check (bank) *cheque* m che-ke
check-in *facturación* f *de equipajes*
fak-too-ra-*thyon* de e-kee-*pa*-khes
cheese *queso* m *ke*-so
chef *cocinero* m ko-thee-*ne*-ro
chemist (pharmacist) *farmacéutico/a* m/f
far-ma-*the*-oo-tee-ko/a
chemist (shop) *farmacia* f far-*ma*-thya
chest *pecho* m *pe*-cho
chicken *pollo* m *po*-lyo
child *niño/a* m/f *nee*-nyo/a
child seat *asiento* m *de seguridad para bebés*
a-*syen*-to de se-goo-ree-*da* pa-ra be-*bes*
childminding service *guardería* f
gwar-de-*ree*-a
children *hijos* m pl *ee*-khos
chilli *guindilla* f geen-*dee*-lya
chocolate *chocolate* m cho-ko-*la*-te
Christian name *nombre* m *de pila* nom-bre
de *pee*-la
Christmas *Navidad* f na-vee-*da*
church *iglesia* f ee-*gle*-sya
cigar *cigarro* m thee-*ga*-ro
cigarette *cigarillo* m thee-ga-*ree*-lyo
cigarette lighter *mechero* m me-*che*-ro
cinema *cine* m *thee*-ne
circus *circo* m *theer*-ko
citizenship *ciudadanía* f
theew-da-da-*nee*-a
city *ciudad* f theew-*da*
city centre *centro* m *de la ciudad* then-tro
de la theew-*da*
classical *clásico/a* m/f *kla*-see-ko/a
clean *limpio/a* m/f *leem*-pyo/a
cleaning *limpieza* f leem-*pye*-tha
client *cliente* m&f klee-*en*-te
cloakroom *guardarropa* m gwar-da-*ro*-pa
close *cerrar* the-*rar*
closed *cerrado/a* m/f the-*ra*-do/a
clothing *ropa* f *ro*-pa
clothing store *tienda* f *de ropa* tyen-da
de *ro*-pa
coast *costa* f *kos*-ta
coffee *café* m ka-*fe*

coins *monedas* f pl mo·ne·das
cold (illness) *resfriado* m res·free·a·do
cold (temperature) *frío/a* m/f free·o/a
colleague *colega* m&f ko·le·ga
collect call *llamada* f a cobro revertido
lya·*ma*·da a ko·bro re·ver·*tee*·do
colour *color* m ko·*lor*
comb *peine* m *pey*·ne
come *venir* ve·*neer*
come (arrive) *llegar* lye·*gar*
comfortable *cómodo/a* m/f *ko*·mo·do/a
companion *compañero/a* m/f
kom·pa·*nye*·ro/a
company *compañía* f kom·pa·*nyee*·a
complain *quejarse* ke·*khar*·se
computer *ordenador* m or·de·na·*dor*
concert *concierto* m kon·*thyer*·to
conditioner *acondicionador* m
a·kon·dee·thyo·na·*dor*
condoms *condones* m pl kon·*do*·nes
confession *confesión* f kon·fe·*syon*
confirm *confirmar* kon·feer·*mar*
connection *conexión* f ko·ne·*ksyon*
constipation *estreñimiento* m
es·tre·nyee·*myen*·to
consulate *consulado* m kon·soo·*la*·do
contact lenses *lentes* m pl *de contacto*
len·tes de kon·*tak*·to
convenience store *negocio* m *de artículos*
básicos ne·*go*·thyo de ar·*tee*·koo·los
ba·see·kos
cook *cocinero* m ko·thee·*ne*·ro
cook *cocinar* ko·thee·*nar*
corkscrew *sacacorchos* m sa·ka·*kor*·chos
cost *costar* kos·*tar*
cotton *algodón* m al·go·*don*
cotton balls *bolas* f pl *de algodón* bo·las
de al·go·*don*
cough *tos* f tos
cough medicine *jarabe* m kha·*ra*·be
countryside *campo* m *kam*·po
court (tennis) *pista* f *pees*·ta
cous cous *cus cus* m koos koos
cover charge *precio* m *del cubierto*
pre·thyo del koo·*byer*·to

crafts *artesanía* f ar·te·sa·*nee*·a
cream *crema* f *kre*·ma
crèche *guardería* f gwar·de·*ree*·a
credit card *tarjeta* f *de crédito* tar·*khe*·ta
de *kre*·dee·to
cup *taza* f *ta*·tha
currency exchange *cambio* m *(de dinero)*
kam·byo (de dee·*ne*·ro)
current (electricity) *corriente* f ko·*ryen*·te
customs *aduana* f a·*dwa*·na
cut *cortar* kor·*tar*
cutlery *cubiertos* m pl koo·*byer*·tos

D

daily *diariamente* dya·rya·*men*·te
dance *bailar* bai·*lar*
dancing *baile* m *bai*·le
dangerous *peligroso/a* m/f pe·lee·*gro*·so/a
dark *oscuro/a* m/f os·*koo*·ro/a
date *citarse* thee·*tar*·se
date (time) *fecha* f *fe*·cha
date of birth *fecha* f *de nacimiento* fe·cha
de na·thee·*myen*·to
daughter *hija* f *ee*·kha
dawn *alba* f *al*·ba
day *día* m *dee*·a
day after tomorrow *pasado mañana*
pa·*sa*·do ma·*nya*·na
day before yesterday *anteayer*
an·te·a·*yer*
delay *demora* f de·*mo*·ra
deliver *entregar* en·tre·*gar*
dental floss *hilo* m *dental* ee·lo den·*tal*
dentist *dentista* m&f den·*tees*·ta
deodorant *desodorante* m de·so·do·*ran*·te
depart *salir de* sa·*leer* de
department store *grandes almacenes* m pl
gran·de al·ma·*then*·es
departure *salida* f sa·*lee*·da
deposit *depósito* m de·*po*·see·to
destination *destino* m des·*tee*·no
diabetes *diabetes* f dee·a·*be*·tes

E English–Spanish dictionary

diaper *pañal* m pa-*nyal*
diaphragm *diafragma* m dee-a-*frag*-ma
diarrhoea *diarrea* f dee-a-*re*-a
diary *agenda* f a-*khen*-da
dictionary *diccionario* m deek-thyo-*na*-ryo
different *diferente* m&f dee-fe-*ren*-te
dining car *vagón* m *restaurante* va-*gon*
res-tow-*ran*-te
dinner *cena* f the-na
direct *directo/a* m/f dee-*rek*-to/a
direct-dial *marcar directo* mar-kar dee-*rek*-to
dirty *sucio/a* m/f *soo*-thyo/a
disabled *minusválido/a* m/f
mee-noos-*va*-lee-do/a
discount *descuento* m des-*kwen*-to
disk *disco* m *dees*-ko
doctor *médico/a* m/f *me*-dee-ko/a
documentary *documental* m
do-koo-men-*tal*
dog *perro/a* m/f *pe*-rro/a
dollar *dólar* m *do*-lar
dope *droga* f *dro*-ga
double bed *cama* f *de matrimonio* ka-ma
de ma-*tree*-mo-nyo
double room *habitación* f *doble*
a-bee-ta-*thyon* do-ble
down *abajo* a-*ba*-kho
dress *vestido* m ves-*tee*-do
drink *bebida* f be-*bee*-da
drink *beber* be-*ber*
drive *conducir* kon-doo-*theer*
drivers licence *carnet* m *de conducir* kar-ne
de kon-doo-*theer*
drug *droga* f *dro*-ga
drunk *borracho/a* m/f bo-*rra*-cho/a
dry *secar* se-*kar*
duck *pato* m *pa*-to
dummy (pacifier) *chupete* m choo-*pe*-te

E

each *cada* ka-da
ear *oreja* f o-*re*-kha
early *temprano* tem-*pra*-no

earplugs *tapones* m pl *para los oídos*
ta-*po*-nes *pa*-ra los o-*ee*-dos
earrings *pendientes* m pl pen-*dyen*-tes
east *este* es-te
Easter *Pascua* f *pas*-kwa
eat *comer* ko-*mer*
economy class *clase* f *turística* kla-se
too-*rees*-tee-ka
electrical store *tienda* f *de productos
eléctricos* tyen-da de pro-*dook*-tos
e-*lek*-tree-kos
electricity *electricidad* f e-lek-tree-thee-*da*
elevator *ascensor* m as-*then*-sor
email *correo* m *electrónico* ko-*re*-o
e-lek-*tro*-nee-ko
embassy *embajada* f em-ba-*kha*-da
emergency *emergencia* f e-mer-*khen*-thya
empty *vacío/a* m/f va-*thee*-o/a
end *acabar* a-ka-*bar*
engagement *compromiso* m
kom-pro-*mee*-so
engine *motor* m mo-*tor*
engineer *ingeniero/a* m/f een-khe-*nye*-ro/a
engineering *ingeniería* f een-khe-*nye-ree*-a
England *Inglaterra* f een-gla-*te*-ra
English *inglés* m een-*gles*
enough *suficiente* m/f soo-fee-*thyen*-te
enter *entrar* en-*trar*
entertainment guide *guía* f *del ocio* gee-a
del o-thyo
envelope *sobre* m *so*-bre
escalator *escaleras* f pl *mecánicas*
es-ka-*le*-ras me-*ka*-nee-kas
Euro *euro* m e-oo-ro
Europe *Europa* f e-oo-*ro*-pa
evening *noche* f *no*-che
everything *todo* to-do
exchange *cambio* m *kam*-byo
exchange (money) *cambiar* kam-*byar*
exchange rate *tipo* m *de cambio* tee-po
de *kam*-byo
exhibition *exposición* f eks-po-see-*thyon*
exit *salida* f sa-*lee*-da

expensive *caro/a* m/f *ka*·ro/a
express mail *correo m urgente* ko·*re*·o
   oor·*khen*·te
eye *ojo* m o·kho

F

face *cara* f *ka*·ra
fall *caída* f ka·ee·da
family *familia* f fa·*mee*·lya
family name *apellido* m a·pe·*lyee*·do
fan (electric) *ventilador* m ven·tee·la·*dor*
fan (hand held) *abanico* m a·ba·*nee*·ko
far *lejos* le·khos
fast *rápido/a* m/f *ra*·pee·do/a
fat *gordo/a* m/f *gor*·do/a
father *padre* m *pa*·dre
father-in-law *suegro* m *swe*·gro
faulty *defectuoso/a* m/f de·fek·too·o·so/a
feel *sentir* sen·*teer*
feelings *sentimientos* m pl sen·tee·*myen*·tos
festival (celebration) *fiesta* f *fyes*·ta
festival (art, music) *festival* m fes·tee·*val*
fever *fiebre* f *fye*·bre
fiancé *prometido* m pro·me·*tee*·do
fiancée *prometida* f pro·me·*tee*·da
film *película* f pe·*lee*·koo·la
film speed *sensibilidad* f sen·see·bee·lee·da
fine *multa* f *mool*·ta
finger *dedo* m *de*·do
first *primero/a* m/f pree·*me*·ro/a
first-aid kit *maletín de primeros auxilios*
   ma·le·*teen* de pree·*me*·ros ow·*ksee*·lyos
first-class *de primera clase* de pree·*me*·ra
   kla·se
fish (live) *pez* m peth
fish (food) *pescado* m pes·*ka*·do
fish shop *pescadería* f pes·ka·de·*ree*·a
fishing *pesca* f *pes*·ka
flashlight *linterna* f leen·*ter*·na
floor *suelo* m *swe*·lo
flower *flor* f flor
fly *volar* vo·*lar*
food *comida* f ko·*mee*·da

foot *pie* m pye
football *fútbol* m *foot*·bol
footpath *acera* f a·*the*·ra
foreign *extranjero/a* m/f eks·tran·*khe*·ro/a
forest *bosque* m *bos*·ke
forever *para siempre* pa·ra *syem*·pre
fork *tenedor* m te·ne·*dor*
fortnight *quincena* f keen·*the*·na
fragile *frágil* *fra*·kheel
free (not bound) *libre* *lee*·bre
free (of charge) *gratis* *gra*·tees
friend *amigo/a* m/f a·*mee*·go/a
frozen foods *productos* m pl *congelados*
   pro·*dook*·tos kon·khe·*la*·dos
fruit *fruta* f *froo*·ta
fry *freír* fre·*eer*
frying pan *sartén* f sar·*ten*
full *lleno/a* m/f *lye*·no/a
funny *gracioso/a* m/f gra·*thyo*·so/a
furniture *muebles* m pl *mwe*·bles
future *futuro* m foo·*too*·ro

G

gasoline *gasolina* f ga·so·*lee*·na
gay *gay* ge
Germany *Alemania* f a·le·*ma*·nya
gift *regalo* m re·*ga*·lo
gig *bolo* m *bo*·lo
girl *chica* f *chee*·ka
girlfriend *novia* f *no*·vya
glass (drinking) *vaso* m *va*·so
glass (material) *vidrio* m *vee*·dree·o
glasses *gafas* f pl *ga*·fas
gloves *guantes* m pl *gwan*·tes
go *ir* eer
go out with *salir con* sa·*leer* kon
go shopping *ir de compras* eer de *kom*·pras
golf course *campo* m *de golf* *kam*·po de golf
good *bueno/a* m/f *bwe*·no/a
gram *gramo* m *gra*·mo
grandchild *nieto/a* m/f *nye*·to/a
grandfather *abuelo* m a·*bwe*·lo
grandmother *abuela* f a·*bwe*·la
gray *gris* grees
great *fantástico/a* m/f fan·*tas*·tee·ko/a

H English–Spanish dictionary

green *verde* ver-de
grey *gris* grees
grocery *tienda* f *de comestibles* tyen-da de ko-mes-tee-bles
grow *crecer* kre-ther
guide (person) *guía* m&f gee-a
guidebook *guía* f gee-a
guided tour *recorrido* m *guiado* re-ko-ree-do gee-a-do

hairdresser *peluquero/a* m/f pe-loo-ke-ro/a
half *medio/a* m/f me-dyo/a
hand *mano* f ma-no
handbag *bolso* m bol-so
handicrafts *artesanía* f ar-te-sa-nee-a
handmade *hecho a mano* e-cho a ma-no
handsome *hermoso/a* m/f er-mo-so/a
happy *feliz* fe-leeth
hard *duro/a* m/f doo-ro/a
hat *sombrero* m som-bre-ro
have *tener* te-ner
hay fever *alergia* f *al polen* a-ler-khya al po-len
he *él* el
head *cabeza* f ka-be-tha
headache *dolor* m *de cabeza* do-lor de ka-be-tha
headlights *faros* m pl fa-ros
heart *corazón* m ko-ra-thon
heart condition *condición* f *cardíaca* kon-dee-thyon kar-dee-a-ka
heat *calor* m ka-lor
heater *estufa* f es-too-fa
heavy *pesado/a* m/f pe-sa-do/a
help *ayudar* a-yoo-dar
her *su* soo
here *aquí* a-kee
high *alto/a* m/f al-to/a
hike *ir de excursión* eer de eks-koor-syon
hiking *excursionismo* m eks-koor-syo-nees-mo
hire *alquilar* al-kee-lar
his *su* soo

hitchhike *hacer dedo* a-ther de-do
holidays *vacaciones* f pl va-ka-thyo-nes
homosexual *homosexual* m&f o-mo-se-kswal
honeymoon *luna* f *de miel* loo-na de myel
hospital *hospital* m os-pee-tal
hot *caliente* ka-lyen-te
hotel *hotel* m o-tel
hungry *tener hambre* te-ner am-bre
husband *marido* m ma-ree-do

I

I *yo* yo
ice *hielo* m ye-lo
ice cream *helado* m e-la-do
identification *identificación* f ee-den-tee-fee-ka-thyon
identification card *carnet* m *de identidad* kar-net de ee-den-tee-da
ill *enfermo/a* m/f en-fer-mo/a
important *importante* eem-por-tan-te
included *incluido* een-kloo-ee-do
indigestion *indigestión* f een-dee-khes-tyon
influenza *gripe* f gree-pe
injection *inyección* f een-yek-thyon
injury *herida* f e-ree-da
insurance *seguro* m se-goo-ro
intermission *descanso* m des-kan-so
internet *internet* m een-ter-net
internet cafe *cibercafe* m thee-ber-ka-fe
interpreter *intérprete* m&f een-ter-pre-te
Ireland *Irlanda* f eer-lan-da
iron *plancha* f plan-cha
island *isla* f ees-la
IT *informática* f een-for-ma-tee-ka
itch *picazón* f pee-ka-thon
itinerary *itinerario* m ee-tee-ne-ra-ryo

J

jacket *chaqueta* f cha-ke-ta
jeans *vaqueros* m pl va-ke-ros

jet lag *jet lag* m dyet lag
jewellery shop *joyería* f kho·ye·*ree*·a
job *trabajo* m tra·*ba*·kho
journalist *periodista* m&f pe·ryo·*dees*·ta
jumper (sweater) *jersey* m *kher*·sey

K

key *llave* f *lya*·ve
kilogram *kilogramo* m kee·lo·gram·o
kilometre *kilómetro* m kee·*lo*·me·tro
kind *amable* a·*ma*·ble
kitchen *cocina* f ko·*thee*·na
knee *rodilla* f ro·*dee*·lya
knife *cuchillo* m koo·*chee*·lyo

L

lake *lago* m *la*·go
languages *idiomas* m pl ee·*dyo*·mas
laptop *ordenador* m *portátil* or·de·na·*dor* por·*ta*·teel
late *tarde* tar·de
laundrette *lavandería* f la·van·de·*ree*·a
laundry *lavadero* m la·va·*de*·ro
law *ley* f ley
lawyer *abogado/a* m/f a·bo·*ga*·do/a
leather *cuero* m *kwe*·ro
left luggage *consigna* f kon·*seeg*·na
leg *pierna* f *pyer*·na
lens *objetivo* m ob·khe·*tee*·vo
lesbian *lesbiana* f les·bee·*a*·na
less *menos* me·nos
letter *carta* f *kar*·ta
library *biblioteca* f bee·blyo·*te*·ka
lifejacket *chaleco* m *salvavidas* cha·*le*·ko sal·va·*vee*·das
lift *ascensor* m as·then·*sor*
light *luz* f looth
light (colour) *claro* *cla*·ro
light (weight) *leve* le·ve
lighter *encendedor* m en·then·de·*dor*
like *gustar(le)* goos·*tar*(le)
line *línea* f *lee*·ne·a
lipstick *pintalabios* m *peen*·ta·la·byos

liquor store *bodega* f bo·*de*·ga
listen *escuchar* es·koo·*char*
local *de cercanías* de ther·ka·*nee*·as
lock *cerradura* f the·ra·*doo*·ra
lock *cerrar* the·*rar*
locked *cerrado/a* m/f *con llave* the·*ra*·do/a kon *lya*·ve
long *largo/a* m/f *lar*·go/a
lost *perdido/a* m/f per·*dee*·do/a
lost property office *oficina* f *de objetos perdidos* o·fee·*thee*·na de ob·*khe*·tos per·*dee*·dos
love *querer* ke·*rer*
lubricant *lubricante* m loo·bree·*kan*·te
luggage *equipaje* m e·kee·*pa*·khe
lunch *almuerzo* m al·*mwer*·tho
luxury *lujo* m *loo*·kho

M

mail *correo* m ko·*re*·o
mailbox *buzón* m boo·*thon*
make-up *maquillaje* m ma·kee·*lya*·khe
man *hombre* m *om*·bre
manager *gerente* m&f *khe*·ren·te
map *mapa* m *ma*·pa
market *mercado* m mer·*ka*·do
marry *casarse* ka·*sar*·se
massage *masaje* m ma·*sa*·khe
masseur/masseuse *masajista* m&f ma·sa·*khees*·ta
match *partido* m par·*tee*·do
matches *cerillas* f pl the·*ree*·lyas
mattress *colchón* m kol·*chon*
measles *sarampión* m sa·ram·*pyon*
meat *carne* f *kar*·ne
medicine *medicina* f me·dee·*thee*·na
menu *menú* m me·*noo*
message *mensaje* m men·*sa*·khe
metre *metro* m *me*·tro
metro station *estación* f *de metro* es·ta·*thyon* de *me*·tro
microwave *microondas* m mee·kro·*on*·das
midnight *medianoche* f me·dya·*no*·che

N English–Spanish dictionary

milk *leche* f *le*·che
millimetre *milímetro* m mee·*lee*·me·tro
mineral water *agua* f *mineral* a·gwa mee·ne·*ral*
minute *minuto* m mee·*noo*·to
mirror *espejo* m es·*pe*·kho
mobile phone *teléfono* m *móvil* te·*le*·fo·no *mo*·veel
modem *módem* m *mo*·dem
moisturiser *crema* f *hidratante* kre·ma ee·dra·*tan*·te
money *dinero* m dee·*ne*·ro
month *mes* m mes
morning (6am–1pm) *mañana* f ma·*nya*·na
mother *madre* f *ma*·dre
mother-in-law *suegra* f *swe*·gra
motorcycle *motocicleta* f mo·to·thee·*kle*·ta
motorway *autovía* f ow·to·*vee*·a
mountain *montaña* f mon·*ta*·nya
mouth *boca* f *bo*·ka
movie *película* f pe·*lee*·koo·la
museum *museo* m moo·*se*·o
music *música* f *moo*·see·ka
musician *músico/a* m/f *moo*·see·ko/a
my *mi* mee

N

nail clippers *cortauñas* m pl kor·ta·*oo*·nyas
name *nombre* m *nom*·bre
name (given) *nombre* m *de pila* nom·bre de *pee*·la
napkin *servilleta* f ser·vee·*lye*·ta
nappy *pañal* m pa·*nyal*
nausea *náusea* f now·se·a
near *cerca* ther·ka
nearby *cerca* ther·ka
nearest *más cercano/a* m/f mas ther·ka·no/a
necklace *collar* m ko·*lyar*
needle (sewing) *aguja* f a·*goo*·kha
Netherlands *Holanda* f o·*lan*·da
new *nuevo/a* m/f *nwe*·vo/a
New Year *Año Nuevo* m a·nyo *nwe*·vo
New Year's Eve *Nochevieja* f no·che·*vye*·kha
New Zealand *Nueva Zelanda* f *nwe*·va the·*lan*·da

news *noticias* f pl no·*tee*·thyas
newsagency *quiosco* m kyos·ko
newspaper *periódico* m pe·*ryo*·dee·ko
next (month) *el próximo (mes)* el *prok*·see·mo (mes)
night *noche* f *no*·che
no *no* no
noisy *ruidoso/a* m/f rwee·*do*·so/a
nonsmoking *no fumadores* no foo·ma·*do*·res
north *norte* m *nor*·te
nose *nariz* f na·*reeth*
notebook *cuaderno* m kwa·*der*·no
nothing *nada* na·da
now *ahora* a·*o*·ra
number *número* m *noo*·me·ro
nurse *enfermero/a* m/f en·fer·*me*·ro/a

O

off (food) *pasado/a* m/f pa·*sa*·do/a
oil *aceite* m a·*they*·te
old *viejo/a* m/f *vye*·kho/a
olive oil *aceite* m *de oliva* a·*they*·te de o·*lee*·va
on *en* en
once *vez* f veth
one-way ticket *billete* m *sencillo* bee·*lye*·te sen·*thee*·lyo
open *abierto/a* m/f a·*byer*·to/a
open *abrir* a·*breer*
opening hours *horas* f pl *de abrir* o·ras de a·*breer*
orange (colour) *naranja* na·*ran*·kha
other *otro/a* m/f *o*·tro/a
our *nuestro/a* m/f *nwes*·tro/a
outside *exterior* m eks·te·*ryor*

P

pacifier (dummy) *chupete* m choo·*pe*·te
package *paquete* m pa·*ke*·te
packet *paquete* m pa·*ke*·te
padlock *candado* m kan·*da*·do

78

pain *dolor* m do·*lor*
painful *doloroso/a* m/f do·lo·*ro*·so/a
painkillers *analgésicos* m pl a·nal·*khe*·see·kos
painter *pintor/pintora* m/f peen·*tor*/peen·*to*·ra
painting *pintura* f peen·*too*·ra
palace *palacio* m pa·*la*·thyo
pants *pantalones* m pl pan·ta·*lo*·nes
panty liners *salvaslips* m pl sal·va·e·*sleeps*
pantyhose *medias* f pl *me*·dyas
paper *papel* m pa·*pel*
paperwork *trabajo* m administrativo tra·*ba*·kho ad·mee·nees·tra·*tee*·vo
parents *padres* m pl *pa*·dres
park *parque* m *par*·ke
park (car) *estacionar* es·ta·thyo·*nar*
party *fiesta* f *fyes*·ta
passenger *pasajero/a* m/f pa·sa·*khe*·ro
passport *pasaporte* m pa·sa·*por*·te
passport number *número* m de pasaporte *noo*·me·ro de pa·sa·*por*·te
past *pasado* m pa·*sa*·do
path *sendero* m sen·*de*·ro
pay *pagar* pa·*gar*
payment *pago* m *pa*·go
pen *bolígrafo* m bo·*lee*·gra·fo
pencil *lápiz* m *la*·peeth
penis *pene* m *pe*·ne
penknife *navaja* f na·*va*·kha
pensioner *pensionista* m&f pen·syo·*nees*·ta
per (day) *por (día)* por (*dee*·a)
perfume *perfume* m per·*foo*·me
petrol *gasolina* f ga·so·*lee*·na
pharmacy *farmacia* f far·*ma*·thya
phone book *guía* f telefónica *gee*·a te·le·*fo*·nee·ka
phone box *cabina* f telefónica ka·*bee*·na te·le·*fo*·nee·ka
phone card *tarjeta* f de teléfono tar·*khe*·ta de te·*le*·fo·no
photograph *foto* f *fo*·to
photograph *sacar fotos* sa·*kar* *fo*·tos

photographer *fotógrafo/a* m/f fo·*to*·gra·fo/a
photography *fotografía* f fo·to·gra·*fee*·a
phrasebook *libro* m de frases *lee*·bro de *fra*·ses
picnic *comida* f en el campo ko·*mee*·da en el *kam*·po
pill *pastilla* f pas·*tee*·lya
pillow *almohada* f al·*mwa*·da
pillowcase *funda* f de almohada *foon*·da de al·*mwa*·da
pink *rosa* *ro*·sa
pistachio *pistacho* m pees·*ta*·cho
plane *avión* m a·*vyon*
plate *plato* m *pla*·to
platform *plataforma* f pla·ta·*for*·ma
play *obra* f *o*·bra
plug *tapar* ta·*par*
point *apuntar* a·poon·*tar*
police *policía* f po·lee·*thee*·a
police station *comisaría* f ko·mee·sa·*ree*·a
pool (swimming) *piscina* f pees·*thee*·na
post code *código postal* m *ko*·dee·go pos·*tal*
post office *correos* m ko·*re*·os
postage *franqueo* m fran·*ke*·o
postcard *postal* f pos·*tal*
poster *póster* m *pos*·ter
pound (money) *libra* f *lee*·bra
pregnant *embarazada* f em·ba·ra·*tha*·da
premenstrual tension *tensión* f premenstrual ten·*syon* pre·mens·*trwal*
price *precio* m *pre*·thyo
private *privado/a* m/f pree·*va*·do/a
pub *pub* m poob
public telephone *teléfono* m público te·*le*·fo·no poo·*blee*·ko
public toilet *servicios* m pl ser·*vee*·thyos
pull *tirar* tee·*rar*
purple *lila* *lee*·la

Q

quiet *tranquilidad* f tran·kee·lee·*da*

R

railway station *estación* f de tren
es·ta·*thyon* de tren
rain *lluvia* f lyoo·vya
raincoat *impermeable* m eem·per·me·*a*·ble
rare *raro/a* m/f *ra*·ro/a
razor *afeitadora* f a·fey·ta·*do*·ra
razor blades *cuchillas* f pl de afeitar
koo·*chee*·lyas de a·fey·*tar*
receipt *recibo* m re·*thee*·bo
recommend *recomendar* re·ko·men·*dar*
red *rojo/a* m/f *ro*·kho/a
refrigerator *nevera* f ne·*ve*·ra • *frigerífico* m
free·ge·*ree*·fee·ko
refund *reembolsar* re·em·bol·*sar*
registered mail *correo* m *certificado*
ko·*re*·o ther·tee·fee·*ka*·do
remote control *mando* m a *distancia*
man·do a dees·*tan*·thya
rent *alquilar* al·kee·*lar*
repair *reparar* re·pa·*rar*
reservation *reserva* f re·*ser*·va
restaurant *restaurante* m res·tow·*ran*·te
return *volver* vol·*ver*
return ticket *billete* m de ida y vuelta
bee·*lye*·te de ee·da ee vwel·ta
right (correct) *correcto/a* m/f ko·*rek*·to/a
right (not left) *derecha* de·*re*·cha
ring *llamar por telefono* lya·*mar* por
te·*le*·fo·no
road *carretera* f ka·re·*te*·ra
rock (music) *rock* m rok
romantic *romántico/a* m/f ro·*man*·tee·ko/a
room *habitación* f a·bee·ta·*thyon*
room number *número* m de la habitación
noo·me·ro de la a·bee·ta·*thyon*
ruins *ruinas* f pl *rwee*·nas

S

safe *caja* f *fuerte* ka·kha *fwer*·te
safe sex *sexo* m *seguro* se·kso se·*goo*·ro
sanitary napkins *compresas* f pl
kom·*pre*·sas

scarf *bufanda* f boo·*fan*·da
school *escuela* f es·*kwe*·la
science *ciencias* f pl *thyen*·thyas
scientist *científico/a* m/f thyen·*tee*·fee·ko/a
scissors *tijeras* f pl tee·*khe*·ras
Scotland *Escocia* f es·*ko*·thya
sculpture *escultura* f es·kool·*too*·ra
sea *mar* m mar
seasick *mareado/a* m/f ma·re·*a*·do/a
season *estación* f es·ta·*thyon*
seat *asiento* m a·*syen*·to
seatbelt *cinturón* m de *seguridad*
theen·too·*ron* de se·goo·ree·*da*
second *segundo/a* m/f se·*goon*·do/a
second *segundo* m se·*goon*·do
second-hand *de segunda mano*
de se·*goon*·da *ma*·no
send *enviar* en·vee·*ar*
service charge *carga* f *kar*·ga
service station *gasolinera* f ga·so·lee·*ne*·ra
sex *sexo* m se·kso
share (a dorm) *compartir (un dormitorio)*
kom·par·*teer* (oon dor·mee·*to*·ryo)
share (with) *compartir* kom·par·*teer*
shave *afeitarse* a·fey·*tar*·se
shaving cream *espuma* f de afeitar
es·*poo*·ma de a·fey·*tar*
sheet (bed) *sábana* f *sa*·ba·na
shirt *camisa* f ka·*mee*·sa
shoe shop *zapatería* f tha·pa·te·*ree*·a
shoes *zapatos* m pl tha·*pa*·tos
shop *tienda* f *tyen*·da
shopping centre *centro* m *comercial*
then·tro ko·mer·*thyal*
short (height) *bajo/a* m/f *ba*·kho/a
short (length) *corto/a* m/f *kor*·to/a
shorts *pantalones* m pl cortos
pan·ta·*lo*·nes *kor*·tos
shoulders *hombros* m pl *om*·bros
shout *gritar* gree·*tar*
show *espectáculo* m es·pek·*ta*·koo·lo
show *mostrar* mos·*trar*
shower *ducha* f *doo*·cha

shut *cerrado/a* m/f the·ra·do/a
sick *enfermo/a* m/f en·fer·mo/a
silk *seda* f se·da
silver *plata* f pla·ta
single *soltero/a* m/f sol·te·ro/a
single room *habitación* f individual a·bee·ta·thyon een·dee·vee·dwal
sister *hermana* f er·ma·na
size (clothes) *talla* f ta·lya
skiing *esquí* m es·kee
skirt *falda* f fal·da
sleep *dormir* dor·meer
sleeping bag *saco* m de dormir sa·ko de dor·meer
sleeping car *coche* m cama ko·che ka·ma
slide *diapositiva* f dya·po·see·tee·va
slowly *despacio* des·pa·thyo
small *pequeño/a* m/f pe·ke·nyo/a
smell *olor* m o·lor
smile *sonreír* son·re·eer
smoke *fumar* foo·mar
snack *tentempié* m ten·tem·pye
snow *nieve* f nye·ve
soap *jabón* m kha·bon
socks *calcetines* m pl kal·the·tee·nes
some *alguno/a* m/f al·goon/al·goo·na
son *hijo* m ee·kho
soon *pronto* pron·to
south *sur* m soor
souvenir *recuerdo* m re·kwer·do
souvenir shop *tienda* f de recuerdos tyen·da de re·kwer·dos
Spain *España* f es·pa·nya
speak *hablar* a·blar
spoon *cuchara* f koo·cha·ra
sports store *tienda* f deportiva tyen·da de·por·tee·va
sprain *torcedura* f tor·the·doo·ra
spring (season) *primavera* f pree·ma·ve·ra
stairway *escalera* f es·ka·le·ra
stamp *sello* m se·lyo
standby ticket *billete* m de lista de espera bee·lye·te de lees·ta de es·pe·ra

station *estación* f es·ta·thyon
stockings *medias* f pl me·dyas
stomach *estómago* m es·to·ma·go
stomach ache *dolor* m de estómago do·lor de es·to·ma·go
stop *parar* pa·rar
street *calle* f ka·lye
string *cuerda* f kwer·da
student *estudiante* m&f es·too·dyan·te
subtitles *subtítulos* m pl soob·tee·too·los
subway *parada* f de metro pa·ra·da de me·tro
suitcase *maleta* f ma·le·ta
summer *verano* m ve·ra·no
sun *sol* m sol
sunblock *crema* f solar kre·ma so·lar
sunburn *quemadura* f de sol ke·ma·doo·ra de sol
sunglasses *gafas* f pl de sol ga·fas de sol
sunrise *amanecer* m a·ma·ne·ther
sunset *puesta* f del sol pwes·ta del sol
supermarket *supermercado* m soo·per·mer·ka·do
surface mail *por vía terrestre* por vee·a te·res·tre
surname *apellido* m a·pe·lyee·do
sweater *jersey* m kher·sey
sweet *dulce* dool·the
swim *nadar* na·dar
swimming pool *piscina* f pees·thee·na
swimsuit *bañador* m ba·nya·dor

T

tailor *sastre* m sas·tre
tampons *tampones* m pl tam·po·nes
tanning lotion *bronceador* m bron·the·a·dor
tap *grifo* m gree·fo
tasty *sabroso/a* m/f sa·bro·so/a
taxi *taxi* m tak·see
taxi stand *parada* f de taxis pa·ra·da de tak·sees

T English–Spanish dictionary

teacher *profesor/profesora* m/f pro·fe·*sor*/pro·fe·*so*·ra

teaspoon *cucharita* f koo·cha·*ree*·ta

telegram *telegrama* m te·le·*gra*·ma

telephone *teléfono* m te·*le*·fo·no

telephone centre *central* f *telefónica* then·*tral* te·le·*fo*·nee·ka

television *televisión* f te·le·vee·*syon*

temperature (fever) *fiebre* f *fye*·bre

temperature (weather) *temperatura* f tem·pe·ra·*too*·ra

tennis *tenis* m *te*·nees

tennis court *pista* f *de tenis* pees·ta de *te*·nees

theatre *teatro* m te·*a*·tro

their *su* soo

thirst *sed* f se

this *éste/a* m/f *es*·te/a

throat *garganta* f gar·*gan*·ta

ticket *billete* m bee·*lye*·te

ticket collector *revisor/revisora* m/f re·vee·*sor*/re·vee·*so*·ra

ticket machine *máquina* f *de billetes* *ma*·kee·na de bee·*lye*·tes

ticket office *taquilla* f ta·*kee*·lya

time (clock) *hora* f o·ra

time (general) *tiempo* m *tyem*·po

time difference *diferencia* f *de horas* dee·fe·*ren*·thya de o·ras

timetable *horario* m o·*ra*·ryo

tin *hojalata* f o·kha·*la*·ta

tin opener *abrelatas* m a·bre·*la*·tas

tip *propina* f pro·*pee*·na

tired *cansado/a* m/f kan·*sa*·do/a

tissues *pañuelos* m pl *de papel* pa·*nywe*·los de pa·*pel*

toast *tostada* f tos·*ta*·da

toaster *tostadora* f tos·ta·*do*·ra

today *hoy* oy

together *juntos/as* m/f pl *khoon*·tos/as

toilet *servicio* m ser·*vee*·thyo

toilet paper *papel* m *higiénico* pa·*pel* ee·*khye*·nee·ko

tomorrow *mañana* ma·*nya*·na

tomorrow afternoon *mañana por la tarde* ma·*nya*·na por la *tar*·de

tomorrow evening *mañana por la noche* ma·*nya*·na por la no·che

tomorrow morning *mañana por la mañana* ma·*nya*·na por la ma·*nya*·na

tone *tono* m *to*·no

tonight *esta noche* es·ta no·che

too (expensive) *demasiado (caro/a)* m/f de·ma·*sya*·do (*ka*·ro/a)

toothache *dolor* m *de muelas* do·*lor* de *mwe*·las

toothbrush *cepillo* m *de dientes* the·*pee*·lyo de *dyen*·tes

toothpaste *pasta* f *dentífrica* pas·ta den·*tee*·free·ka

toothpick *palillo* m pa·*lee*·lyo

torch *linterna* f leen·*ter*·na

tour *excursión* f eks·koor·*syon*

tourist *turista* m&f too·*rees*·ta

tourist office *oficina* f *de turismo* o·fee·*thee*·na de too·*rees*·mo

towel *toalla* f to·*a*·lya

tower *torre* f *to*·re

traffic *tráfico* m *tra*·fee·ko

traffic lights *semáforos* m pl se·*ma*·fo·ros

train *tren* m tren

train station *estación* f *de tren* es·ta·*thyon* de tren

tram *tranvía* m tran·*vee*·a

transit lounge *sala* f *de tránsito* *sa*·la de *tran*·see·to

translate *traducir* tra·doo·*theer*

travel agency *agencia* f *de viajes* a·*khen*·thya de *vya*·khes

travel sickness *mareo* m ma·*re*·o

travellers cheque *cheques* m pl *de viajero* *che*·kes de vya·*khe*·ro

trousers *pantalones* m pl pan·ta·*lo*·nes

try *probar* pro·*bar*

T-shirt *camiseta* f ka·mee·*se*·ta

tube (tyre) *cámara* f *de aire* ka·ma·ra de *ai*·re

TV *tele* f te·le
tweezers *pinzas* f pl *peen*·thas
twin beds *dos camas* f pl dos *ka*·mas
tyre *neumático* m ne·oo·*ma*·tee·ko

U

umbrella *paraguas* m pa·ra·gwas
uncomfortable *incómodo/a* m/f
  een·*ko*·mo·do/a
underpants (men) *calzoncillos* m pl
  kal·thon·*thee*·lyos
underpants (women) *bragas* f pl *bra*·gas
underwear *ropa interior* f ro·pa een·te·*ryor*
university *universidad* f oo·nee·ver·see·*da*
until (June) *hasta (junio)* as·ta (*khoo*·nyo)
up *arriba* a·*ree*·ba
urgent *urgente* oor·*khen*·te
USA *Los Estados* m pl *Unidos* los es·*ta*·dos
  oo·*nee*·dos

V

vacant *vacante* va·*kan*·te
vacation *vacaciones* f pl va·ka·*thyo*·nes
vaccination *vacuna* f va·*koo*·na
validate *validar* va·lee·*dar*
vegetable *verdura* f ver·*doo*·ra
vegetarian *vegetariano/a* m/f
  ve·khe·ta·*rya*·no/a
video tape *cinta* f *de vídeo* theen·ta de
  vee·de·o
view *vista* f *vees*·ta
village *pueblo* m *pwe*·blo
visa *visado* m vee·*sa*·do

W

wait *esperar* es·pe·*rar*
waiter *camarero/a* m/f ka·ma·*re*·ro/a
waiting room *sala* f *de espera* sa·la de
  es·*pe*·ra
walk *caminar* ka·mee·*nar*
wallet *cartera* f kar·*te*·ra
warm *templado/a* m/f tem·*pla*·do/a

wash (something) *lavar* la·*var*
washing machine *lavadora* f la·va·*do*·ra
watch *reloj* m *de pulsera* re·*lokh* de
  pool·*se*·ra
water *agua* f *a*·gwa
wedding *boda* f *bo*·da
weekend *fin de semana* m feen de se·*ma*·na
west *oeste* m o·*es*·te
wheelchair *silla* f *de ruedas* see·lya de
  rwe·das
when *cuando* kwan·do
where *donde/dónde* don·de
white *blanco/a* m/f blan·ko/a
who *quien* kyen
why *por qué* por ke
wife *esposa* f es·*po*·sa
window *ventana* f ven·*ta*·na
wine *vino* m vee·no
with *con* kon
without *sin* seen
woman *mujer* f moo·*kher*
wood *madera* f ma·*de*·ra
wool *lana* f *la*·na
world *mundo* m moon·do
World Cup *La Copa Mundial* f la *ko*·pa
  moon·*dyal*
write *escribir* es·kree·*beer*

Y

yellow *amarillo/a* m/f a·ma·*ree*·lyo/a
yes *sí* see
yesterday *ayer* a·*yer*
you pol sg *Usted* oos·*te*
you inf sg *tú* too
you pol pl *ustedes* oos·*te*·des
you inf pl *vosotros* vo·*so*·tros
youth hostel *albergue* m *juvenil* al·*ber*·ge
  khoo·ve·*neel*

Z

zodiac *zodíaco* m tho·*dee*·a·ko
zoo *zoológico* m zo·o·*lo*·khee·ko

A Spanish—English dictionary

Nouns in this dictionary have their gender indicated by m (masculine) or f (feminine).
If it's a plural noun, you'll also see pl.
Where no gender is marked the word is either an adjective or a verb, with adjectives first.

A

a bordo a *bor*·do *aboard*
abajo a·*ba*·kho *down*
abierto/a m/f a·*byer*·to/a *open*
abogado/a m/f a·bo·*ga*·do/a *lawyer*
abrebotellas m a·bre·bo·te·lyas *bottle opener*
abrelatas m a·bre·*la*·tas *can opener*
abuela f a·*bwe*·la *grandmother*
abuelo m a·*bwe*·lo *grandfather*
aburrido/a m/f a·boo·ree·do/a *boring*
accidente m ak·thee·*den*·te *accident*
aceite m a·*they*·te *oil*
— **de oliva** de o·*lee*·va *olive oil*
acondicionador m a·kon·dee·thyo·na·*dor* *conditioner*
adaptador m a·dap·ta·*dor* *adaptor*
aduana f a·*dwa*·na *customs*
aerolínea f ay·ro·*lee*·nya *airline*
aeropuerto m ay·ro·*pwer*·to *airport*
afeitadora f a·fey·ta·*do*·ra *razor*
agencia f **de viajes** a·*khen*·thya de *vya*·khes *travel agency*
agua f *a*·gwa *water*
— **mineral** mee·ne·*ral* *mineral water*
ahora a·*o*·ra *now*
alba f *al*·ba *dawn*
albergue m **juvenil** al·*ber*·ge khoo·ve·*neel* *youth hostel*
Alemania f a·le·*ma*·nya *Germany*
alegría f a·le·*gree*·a *happiness*
alergia f a·*ler*·khya *allergy*
— **al polen** al *po*·len *hay fever*
algodón m al·go·*don* *cotton*
alguno/a m/f al·*goon*/al·*goo*·na *some*
almuerzo m al·*mwer*·tho *lunch*
alojamiento m a·lo·kha·*myen*·to *accommodation*

alquilar al·kee·*lar* *hire*
alto/a m/f *al*·to/a *high*
amable a·*ma*·ble *kind*
amanecer m a·ma·ne·*ther* *sunrise*
ampolla f am·*po*·lya *blister*
analgésicos m pl a·nal·*khe*·see·kos *painkillers*
Año Nuevo m *a*·nyo *nwe*·vo *New Year*
anteayer an·te·a·*yer* *day before yesterday*
antibióticos m pl an·tee·*byo*·tee·kos *antibiotics*
antigüedad f an·tee·gwe·*da* *antique*
antiséptico m an·tee·*sep*·tee·ko *antiseptic*
apellido m a·pe·*lyee*·do *family name*
aquí a·*kee* *here*
arte m *ar*·te *art*
artesanía f ar·te·sa·*nee*·a *crafts*
ascensor m as·then·*sor* *elevator* • *lift*
asiento m a·*syen*·to *seat*
aspirina f as·pee·*ree*·na *aspirin*
autobús m ow·to·*boos* *bus (local)*
autocar m ow·to·*kar* *bus (intercity)*
autovia f ow·to·*vee*·a *motorway*
avión m a·*vyon* *plane*
ayer a·*yer* *yesterday*

B

bailar m bai·*lar* *dancing*
bajo/a m/f *ba*·kho/a *short (height)*
bañador m ba·nya·*dor* *swimsuit*
bañera f ba·*nye*·ra *bath*
baño m *ba*·nyo *bathroom*
barato/a m/f ba·*ra*·to/a *cheap*
bebida f be·*bee*·da *drink*

biblioteca f bee-blyo-te-ka *library*
billete m bee-lye-te *ticket*
— **de ida y vuelta** de ee-da ee vwel-ta *return ticket*
— **sencillo** sen-thee-lyo *one-way ticket*
blanco y negro blan-ko ee ne-gro *B&W (film)*
boca f bo-ka *mouth*
boda f bo-da *wedding*
bodega f bo-de-ga *liquor store*
bolígrafo m bo-lee-gra-fo *pen*
bolso m bol-so *bag • handbag*
bosque m bos-ke *forest*
botella f bo-te-lya *bottle*
brazo m bra-tho *arm*
bueno/a m/f bwe-no/a *good*

C

cabeza f ka-be-tha *head*
cada ka-da *each*
café m ka-fe *café • coffee*
caja f ka-kha *box*
— **fuerte** fwer-te *safe*
— **registradora** re-khees-tra-do-ra *cash register*
cajero m **automático** ka-khe-ro ow-to-ma-tee-ko *automatic teller machine (ATM)*
caliente ka-lyen-te *hot*
calle f ka-lye *street*
calor m ka-lor *heat*
cama f ka-ma *bed*
— **de matrimonio** de ma-tree-mo-nyo *double bed*
cámara f **(fotográfica)** ka-ma-ra (fo-to-gra-fee-ka) *camera*
cámara f **de aire** ka-ma-ra de ai-re *tube (tyre)*
camarero/a m/f ka-ma-re-ro/a *waiter*
cambiar kam-byar *change • exchange (money)*
— **(un cheque)** (oon che-ke) *cash (a cheque)*

cambio m kam-byo *change (money) • currency exchange • exchange*
caminar ka-mee-nar *walk*
camisa f ka-mee-sa *shirt*
camiseta f ka-mee-se-ta *T-shirt*
cámping m kam-peen *campsite*
campo m kam-po *countryside*
— **de golf** de golf *golf course*
cancelar kan-the-lar *cancel*
candado m kan-da-do *padlock*
canguros m kan-goo-ros *babysitter*
cansado/a m/f kan-sa-do/a *tired*
cara f ka-ra *face*
carga f kar-ga *service charge*
carne f kar-ne *meat*
carnet m **de conducir** kar-ne de kon-doo-theer *drivers licence*
carnet m **de identidad** kar-net de ee-den-tee-da *identification card*
carnicería f kar-nee-the-ree-a *butcher's shop*
caro/a m/f ka-ro/a *expensive*
carta f kar-ta *letter*
castillo m kas-tee-lyo *castle*
catedral f ka-te-dral *cathedral*
cena f the-na *dinner*
centro m then-tro *centre*
— **comercial** ko-mer-thyal *shopping centre*
— **de la ciudad** de la theew-da *city centre*
cerca ther-ka *near • nearby*
cerrado/a m/f ther-ra-do/a *closed*
— **con llave** kon lya-ve *locked*
cerradura f the-ra-doo-ra *lock*
cerrar the-rar *close • lock*
cerveza f ther-ve-tha *beer*
chaqueta f cha-ke-ta *jacket*
cheque m che-ke *check (bank)*
cheques m pl **de viajero** che-kes de vya-khe-ro *travellers cheque*

chica f *chee·ka girl*
chico m *chee·ko boy*
cibercafé thee·ber·ka·fe *internet café*
cigarrillo m thee·ga·ree·lyo *cigarette*
cigarro m thee·*ga·ro cigar*
cine m *thee·ne cinema*
circo m *theer·ko circus*
ciudad f theew·*da city*
clase f **preferente** *kla·se pre·fe·ren·te
business class*
clase f **turística** *kla·se too·rees·tee·ka
economy class*
coche m **cama** *ko·che ka·ma sleeping car*
coche m *ko·che car*
cocina f ko·*thee·na kitchen*
cocinar ko·thee·*nar cook*
cocinero m ko·thee·*ne·ro cook*
código m **postal** *ko·dee·go pos·tal
post code*
comer ko·*mer eat*
comerciante m&f ko·mer·*thyan·te
business person*
comida f ko·*mee·da food*
comisaría f ko·mee·sa·*ree·a police station*
cómodo/a m/f ko·mo·do/a *comfortable*
cómpact m *kom·pakt CD*
compañero/a m/f kom·pa·*nye·ro/a
companion*
compartir kom·par·*teer share (with)*
comprar kom·*prar buy*
con kon *with*
concierto m kon·*thyer·to concert*
condición f **cardíaca** kon·dee·*thyon
kar·dee·a·ka heart condition*
conducir kon·doo·*theer drive*
consigna f kon·*seeg·na left luggage*
consulado m kon·soo·*la·do consulate*
corazón m ko·ra·*thon heart*

correo m ko·*re·o mail*
— **certificado** ther·tee·fee·*ka·do
registered mail*
— **urgente** oor·*khen·te express mail*
correos ko·*re·os post office*
corrida f ko·*ree·da bullfight*
cortar kor·*tar cut*
corto/a m/f *kor·to/a short*
costar kos·*tar cost*
crema *kre·ma cream*
— **hidratante** ee·dra·*tan·te moisturiser*
— **solar** so·*lar sunblock*
cuaderno m kwa·*der·no notebook*
cuando *kwan·do when*
cubiertos m pl koo·*byer·tos cutlery*
cuchara f koo·*cha·ra spoon*
cucharita f koo·cha·*ree·ta teaspoon*
cuchillo m koo·*chee·lyo knife*
cuenta f *kwen·ta bill*
— **bancaria** ban·*ka·rya bank account*
cuero m *kwe·ro leather*
cumpleaños m koom·ple·*a·nyos birthday*

D

dedo m *de·do finger*
defectuoso/a m/f de·fek·too·*o·so/a
faulty*
demasiado (caro/a) m/f de·ma·*sya·do
(ka·ro/a) *too (expensive)*
derecha de·*re·cha right (not left)*
desayuno m des·a·*yoo·no breakfast*
descanso m des·*kan·so intermission*
descuento m des·*kwen·to discount*
despacio des·*pa·thyo slowly*
despertador m des·per·ta·*dor alarm clock*
después de des·*pwes de after*
detrás de de·*tras de behind*
día m *dee·a day*
diapositiva f dya·po·see·*tee·va slide*
diariamente dya·rya·*men·te daily*

dinero m dee-*ne*-ro *money*
— **en efectivo** en e-*fek*-*tee*-vo *cash*
dirección f dee-rek-*thyon address*
disco m *dees*-ko *disk*
documental m do-koo-men-*tal documentary*
dólar m do-*lar dollar*
dolor m do-*lor pain*
— **de cabeza** de ka-*be*-tha *headache*
— **de estómago** de es-*to*-ma-go *stomach ache*
— **de muelas** de *mwe*-las *toothache*
donde *don*-de *where*
dormir dor-*meer sleep*
dos camas f pl dos *ka*-mas *twin beds*
droga f dro-ga *drug*
ducha f *doo*-cha *shower*
dulce *dool*-the *sweet*
duro/a m/f *doo*-ro/a *hard*

E

edificio m e-dee-*fee*-thyo *building*
embajada f em-ba-*kha*-da *embassy*
embarazada f em-ba-ra-*tha*-da *pregnant*
en en *on*
enfermero/a m/f en-fer-*me*-ro/a *nurse*
enfermo/a m/f en-*fer*-mo/a *sick*
entrar en-*trar enter*
enviar en-vee-*ar send*
equipaje m e-kee-*pa*-khe *luggage*
escalera f es-ka-*le*-ra *stairway*
Escocia f es-*ko*-thya *Scotland*
escribir es-kree-*beer write*
escuchar es-koo-*char listen*
escuela f es-*kwe*-la *school*
espalda f es-*pal*-da *back (of body)*
espectáculo m es-pek-*ta*-koo-lo *show*
esperar es-pe-*rar wait*
esposa f es-*po*-sa *wife*
espuma de afeitar es-*poo*-ma de a-*fey*-tar *shaving cream*

esquí m es-*kee skiing*
esta noche es-ta *no*-che *tonight*
éste/a m/f es-te/a *this*
estación f es-ta-*thyon season • station*
— **de autobuses** f de ow-to-*boo*-ses *bus station (local)*
— **de autocares** f de ow-to-*ka*-res *bus station (intercity)*
— **de metro** de *me*-tro *metro station*
— **de tren** de tren *railway station*
estacionar es-ta-thyo-*nar park (car)*
estómago m es-*to*-ma-go *stomach*
estudiante m&f es-too-*dyan*-te *student*
excursión f eks-koor-*syon tour*
excursionismo m eks-koor-syo-*nees*-mo *hiking*
exposición f eks-po-see-*thyon exhibition*
extranjero/a m/f eks-tran-*khe*-ro/a *foreign*

F

facturación f de equipajes fak-too-ra-*thyon* de e-kee-*pa*-khes *check-in*
falda f *fal*-da *skirt*
farmacia f far-*ma*-thya *pharmacy*
fecha f *fe*-cha *date (time)*
— **de nacimiento** de na-thee-*myen*-to *date of birth*
fiebre f *fye*-bre *temperature (fever)*
fiesta f *fyes*-ta *party*
foto f *fo*-to *photo*
fotógrafo/a m/f fo-*to*-gra-fo/a *photographer*
frágil fra-*kheel fragile*
frenos m pl *fre*-nos *brakes*
frío/a m/f *free*-o/a *cold*
frontera f fron-*te*-ra *border*
fruta f *froo*-ta *fruit*
fumar foo-*mar smoke*

G

gafas f pl *ga*·fas *glasses*
— **de sol** de sol *sunglasses*
garganta f gar·*gan*·ta *throat*
gasolina f ga·so·*lee*·na *petrol*
gasolinera f ga·so·lee·*ne*·ra *service station*
gay ge *gay*
gerente m&f khe·*ren*·te *manager*
gordo/a m/f *gor*·do/a *fat*
grande *gran*·de *big*
grandes almacenes m pl *gran*·des al·ma·*then*·es *department store*
gratis *gra*·tees *free (of charge)*
grifo m *gree*·fo *tap*
gripe f *gree*·pe *influenza*
gris grees *grey*
guardarropa m gwar·da·*ro*·pa *cloakroom*
guardería f gwar·de·*ree*·a *childminding service*
guía m&f *gee*·a *guide (person)*
guía f *gee*·a *guidebook*

H

habitación f a·bee·ta·*thyon* *bedroom • room*
— **doble** *do*·ble *double room*
— **individual** een·dee·vee·*dwal* *single room*
hablar a·*blar* *speak*
helado m e·*la*·do *ice cream*
hermana f er·*ma*·na *sister*
hermano m er·*ma*·no *brother*
hermoso/a m/f er·*mo*·so/a *beautiful*
hielo m *ye*·lo *ice*
hija f *ee*·kha *daughter*
hijo m *ee*·kho *son*
hijos m pl *ee*·khos *children*
hombre m *om*·bre *man*
hombros m pl *om*·bros *shoulders*
hora f *o*·ra *time*
horario m o·*ra*·ryo *timetable*
hoy oy *today*

I

idiomas m pl ee·*dyo*·mas *languages*
iglesia f ee·*gle*·sya *church*
impermeable m eem·per·me·*a*·ble *raincoat*
incluido een·kloo·*ee*·do *included*
informática f een·for·*ma*·tee·ka *IT*
ingeniería f een·khe·nye·*ree*·a *engineering*
Inglaterra f een·gla·*te*·ra *England*
inglés m een·*gles* *English*
ir eer *go*
ir de compras eer de *kom*·pras *go shopping*
ir de excursión eer de eks·koor·*syon* *hike*
isla f *ees*·la *island*

J

jabón m kha·*bon* *soap*
joyería f kho·ye·*ree*·a *jewellery shop*
juntos/as m/f pl *khoon*·tos/as *together*

L

lago m *la*·go *lake*
lana f *la*·na *wool*
lápiz m *la*·peeth *pencil*
largo/a m/f *lar*·go/a *long*
lavadero m la·va·*de*·ro *laundry*
lavandería f la·van·de·*ree*·a *laundrette*
lavar la·*var* *wash (something)*
leche f *le*·che *milk*
lejos *le*·khos *far*
libra f *lee*·bra *pound (money)*
libre *lee*·bre *free (not bound)*
librería f lee·bre·*ree*·a *bookshop*
libro m *lee*·bro *book*
limpieza f leem·*pye*·tha *cleaning*
llave f *lya*·ve *key*
llegadas f pl lye·*ga*·das *arrivals*
llegar lye·*gar* *come (arrive)*

lleno/a m/f *lye*-no/a *booked out • full*

Los Estados Unidos m pl los es-*ta*-dos oo-*nee*-dos *USA*

luz f looth *light*

M

madre f *ma*-dre *mother*

maleta f ma-*le*-ta *suitcase*

malo/a m/f *ma*-lo/a *bad*

mano f *ma*-no *hand*

manta f *man*-ta *blanket*

mapa m *ma*-pa *map*

maquillaje m ma-kee-*lya*-khe *make-up*

marido m ma-*ree*-do *husband*

matrícula f ma-*tree*-koo-la *car registration*

medias f pl *me*-dyas *pantyhose • stockings*

medio/a m/f *me*-dyo/a *half*

mejor me-*khor* *better*

mercado m mer-*ka*-do *market*

minusválido/a m/f mee-noos-*va*-lee-do/a *disabled*

mochila f mo-*chee*-la *backpack*

monedas f pl mo-*ne*-das *coins*

montaña f mon-*ta*-nya *mountain*

motocicleta f mo-to-thee-*kle*-ta *motorcycle*

muebles m pl *mwe*-bles *furniture*

mujer f moo-*kher* *woman*

multa f *mool*-ta *fine*

museo m moo-*se*-o *museum*

— **de arte** de *ar*-te *art gallery*

N

nada *na*-da *nothing*

nadar na-*dar* *swim*

nariz f na-*reeth* *nose*

navaja f na-*va*-kha *penknife*

Navidad f na-vee-*da* *Christmas*

negocio m de artículos básicos ne-*go*-thyo de ar-*tee*-koo-los *ba*-see-kos *convenience store*

negocios m pl ne-*go*-thyos *business*

neumático m ne-oo-*ma*-tee-ko *tyre*

nevera f ne-*ve*-ra *refrigerator*

nieto/a m/f *nye*-to/a *grandchild*

nieve f *nye*-ve *snow*

niño/a m/f *nee*-nyo/a *child*

no fumadores no foo-ma-*do*-res *nonsmoking*

noche f *no*-che *evening • night*

Nochevieja f no-che-*vye*-kha *New Year's Eve*

nombre m *nom*-bre *name*

— **de pila** de *pee*-la *first/given name*

norte m *nor*-te *north*

noticias f pl no-*tee*-thyas *news*

novia f *no*-vya *girlfriend*

novio m *no*-vyo *boyfriend*

nuestro/a m/f *nwes*-tro/a *our*

Nueva Zelanda f *nwe*-va the-*lan*-da *New Zealand*

nuevo/a m/f *nwe*-vo/a *new*

número m *noo*-me-ro *number*

O

objetivo m ob-khe-*tee*-vo *lens*

obra f *o*-bra *play*

ocupado/a m/f o-koo-*pa*-do/a *busy*

oeste m o-*es*-te *west*

oficina f o-fee-*thee*-na *office*

— **de objetos perdidos** de ob-*khe*-tos per-*dee*-dos *lost property office*

— **de turismo** de too-*rees*-mo *tourist office*

ojo m *o*-kho *eye*

olor m o-*lor* *smell*

ordenador m or-de-na-*dor* *computer*

— **portátil** por-*ta*-teel *laptop*

oreja f o-*re*-kha *ear*

oscuro/a m/f os-*koo*-ro/a *dark*

otra vez *o*-tra veth *again*

SPA - ENG **LOOK UP**

otro/a m/f *o·*tro/a *other*

P

padre m *pa·*dre *father*
padres m pl *pa·*dres *parents*
pagar pa·*gar* *pay*
pago m *pa·*go *payment*
palacio m pa·*la·*thyo *palace*
pan m pan *bread*
panadería f pa·na·de·*ree·*a *bakery*
pañal m pa·*nyal* *diaper • nappy*
pantalones m pl pan·ta·*lo·*nes *trousers*
— cortos *kor·*tos *shorts*
pañuelos m pl de papel pa·*nywe·*los de pa·*pel* *tissues*
papel m pa·*pel* *paper*
— higiénico ee·*khye·*nee·ko *toilet paper*
papeles m pl del coche pa·*pe·*les del *ko·*che *car owner's title*
paquete m pa·*ke·*te *package • packet*
parada f pa·*ra·*da *stop*
— de autobús ow·to·*boos* *bus stop*
— de taxis tak·*sees* *taxi stand*
paraguas m pa·*ra·*gwas *umbrella*
parar pa·*rar* *stop*
parque m *par·*ke *park*
pasado m pa·*sa·*do *past*
pasajero/a m/f pa·sa·*khe·*ro *passenger*
pasaporte m pa·sa·*por·*te *passport*
Pascua f *pas·*kwa *Easter*
pastelería f pas·te·le·*ree·*a *cake shop*
pastilla f pas·*tee·*lya *pill*
pato m *pa·*to *duck*
pecho m *pe·*cho *chest*
película f pe·*lee·*koo·la *movie*
peligroso/a m/f pe·lee·*gro·*so/a *dangerous*
peluquero/a m/f pe·loo·*ke·*ro/a *hairdresser*
pensión f pen·*syon* *boarding house*

pensionista m&f pen·syo·*nees·*ta *pensioner*
pequeño/a m/f pe·*ke·*nyo/a *small*
perdido/a m/f per·*dee·*do/a *lost*
periódico m pe·*ryo·*dee·ko *newspaper*
periodista m&f pe·ryo·*dees·*ta *journalist*
pesca f *pes·*ka *fishing*
pescadería f pes·ka·de·*ree·*a *fish shop*
pescado m pes·*ka·*do *fish (food)*
pez m peth *fish (live)*
pie m pye *foot*
pierna f *pyer·*na *leg*
pila f *pee·*la *battery*
pintalabios m *peen·*ta·la·byos *lipstick*
pintor/pintora m/f peen·*tor*/peen·*to·*ra *painter*
pintura f peen·*too·*ra *painting*
piscina f pees·*thee·*na *swimming pool*
plancha f *plan·*cha *iron*
plata f *pla·*ta *silver*
playa f *pla·*ya *beach*
plaza f de toros *pla·*tha de *to·*ros *bullring*
policía f po·lee·*thee·*a *police*
pollo m *po·*lyo *chicken*
postal f pos·*tal* *postcard*
precio m *pre·*thyo *price*
— de entrada de en·*tra·*da *admission price*
— del cubierto del koo·*byer·*to *cover charge*
primavera f pree·ma·*ve·*ra *spring (season)*
primero/a m/f pree·*me·*ro/a *first*
privado/a m/f pree·*va·*do/a *private*
probar pro·*bar* *try*
productos alimentarios m pl pro·*dook·*tos a·lee·men·*ta·*ryos *foodstuffs*
productos congelados m pl pro·*dook·*tos kon·khe·*la·*dos *frozen foods*
profesor/profesora m/f pro·fe·*sor*/pro·fe·*so·*ra *teacher*
prometida f pro·me·*tee·*da *fiancée*
prometido m pro·me·*tee·*do *fiancé*
pronto *pron·*to *soon*

Spanish–English dictionary Q

propina f pro·*pee*·na *tip*
pub m poob *bar (with music)*
pueblo m *pwe*·blo *village*
puente m *pwen*·te *bridge*
puesta f del sol *pwes*·ta del sol *sunset*

Q

quemadura f ke·ma·*doo*·ra *burn*
— **de sol** de sol *sunburn*
queso m *ke*·so *cheese*
quien kyen *who*
quincena f keen·*the*·na *fortnight*
quiosco m *kyos*·ko *newsagency*

R

rápido/a m/f *ra*·pee·do/a *fast*
raro/a m/f *ra*·ro/a *rare*
recibo m re·*thee*·bo *receipt*
recorrido m guiado re·ko·*ree*·do gee·*a*·do *guided tour*
recuerdo m re·*kwer*·do *souvenir*
reembolsar re·em·bol·*sar* *refund*
regalo m re·*ga*·lo *gift*
reloj m de pulsera re·*lokh* de pool·*se*·ra *watch*
reserva f re·*ser*·va *reservation*
reservar re·ser·*var* *book (make a reservation)*
resfriado m res·*free*·a·do *cold (illness)*
rodilla f ro·*dee*·lya *knee*
ropa f *ro*·pa *clothing*
— **de cama** de *ka*·ma *bedding*
— **interior** een·te·*ryor* *underwear*
roto/a m/f *ro*·to/a *broken*
ruidoso/a m/f rwee·*do*·so/a *noisy*
ruinas f pl *rwee*·nas *ruins*

S

sábana f *sa*·ba·na *sheet (bed)*
sabroso/a m/f sa·*bro*·so/a *tasty*

saco m de dormir *sa*·ko de dor·*meer* *sleeping bag*
sala f *sa*·la *auditorium, hall • living room*
— **de espera** de es·*pe*·ra *waiting room*
— **de tránsito** de *tran*·see·to *transit lounge*
salida f sa·*lee*·da *exit*
salir con sa·*leer* kon *go out with*
salir de sa·*leer* de *depart*
salón m de belleza sa·*lon* de be·*lye*·tha *beauty salon*
sangre f *san*·gre *blood*
sastre m *sas*·tre *tailor*
seda f *se*·da *silk*
segundo m se·*goon*·do *second*
segundo/a m/f se·*goon*·do/a *second*
seguro m se·*goo*·ro *insurance*
sello m *se*·lyo *stamp*
semáforos m pl se·*ma*·fo·ros *traffic lights*
sendero m sen·*de*·ro *path*
servicio m ser·*vee*·thyo *toilet*
servicios m pl ser·*vee*·thyos *public toilet*
sexo m *se*·kso *sex*
— **seguro** se·*goo*·ro *safe sex*
silla f *see*·lya *chair*
— **de ruedas** de *rwe*·das *wheelchair*
sin seen *without*
sobre m *so*·bre *envelope*
sol m sol *sun*
solo/a m/f *so*·lo/a *alone*
soltero/a m/f sol·*te*·ro/a *single*
sombrero m som·*bre*·ro *hat*
subtítulos m pl soob·*tee*·too·los *subtitles*
sucio/a m/f *soo*·thyo/a *dirty*
suegra f *swe*·gra *mother-in-law*
suegro m *swe*·gro *father-in-law*
sujetador m soo·khe·ta·*dor* *bra*
supermercado m soo·per·mer·*ka*·do *supermarket*
sur m soor *south*

T

talla f *ta*-lya *size (clothes)*
taquilla f ta-*kee*-lya *ticket office*
tarde *tar*-de *late*
tarjeta f tar-*khe*-ta *card*
— **de crédito** de *kre*-dee-to *credit card*
— **de embarque** de em-*bar*-ke *boarding pass*
— **de teléfono** de te-*le*-fo-no *phone card*
tasa f **(del aeropuerto)** *ta*-sa (del ay-ro-*pwer*-to) *(airport tax)*
teatro m te-*a*-tro *theatre*
tele f *te*-le *TV*
teléfono m te-*le*-fo-no *telephone*
— **móvil** *mo*-veel *mobile phone*
— **público** *poo*-blee-ko *public telephone*
templado/a m/f tem-*pla*-do/a *warm*
temprano tem-*pra*-no *early*
tenedor m te-ne-*dor* *fork*
tentempié m ten-tem-*pye* *snack*
tía f *tee*-a *aunt*
tienda f *tyen*-da *shop*
— **de comestibles** de ko-mes-*tee*-bles *grocery store*
— **de recuerdos** de re-*kwer*-dos *souvenir shop*
— **de ropa** de *ro*-pa *clothing store*
— **deportiva** de-por-*tee*-va *sports store*
tijeras f pl tee-*khe*-ras *scissors*
tipo m **de cambio** *tee*-po de *kam*-byo *exchange rate*
tirar tee-*rar* *pull*
toalla f to-*a*-lya *towel*
tobillo m to-*bee*-lyo *ankle*
todo *to*-do *all • everything*
torcedura f tor-the-*doo*-ra *sprain*
toro m *to*-ro *bull*
torre f *to*-re *tower*
tos f tos *cough*
tostada f tos-*ta*-da *toast*
tostadora f tos-ta-*do*-ra *toaster*

trabajo m tra-*ba*-kho *job*
traducir tra-doo-*theer* *translate*
tranquilidad f tran-kee-lee-*da* *quiet*
tranvía m tran-*vee*-a *tram*
tren m tren *train*
turista m&f too-*rees*-ta *tourist*

U

universidad f oo-nee-ver-see-*da* *university*
urgente oor-*khen*-te *urgent*

V

vacaciones f pl va-ka-*thyo*-nes *holidays • vacation*
vacío/a m/f va-*thee*-o/a *empty*
vacuna f va-*koo*-na *vaccination*
validar va-lee-*dar* *validate*
vaqueros m pl va-*ke*-ros *jeans*
vaso m *va*-so *glass (drinking)*
venir ve-*neer* *come*
ventana f ven-*ta*-na *window*
ventilador m ven-tee-la-*dor* *fan (electric)*
verano m ve-*ra*-no *summer*
verdura f ver-*doo*-ra *vegetable*
vestido m ves-*tee*-do *dress*
vestuarios m pl ves-*twa*-ryos *changing rooms*
viejo/a m/f *vye*-kho/a *old*
vino m *vee*-no *wine*
volver vol-*ver* *return*

Z

zapatería f tha-pa-te-*ree*-a *shoe shop*
zapatos m pl tha-*pa*-tos *shoes*

What kind of traveller are you?

A. You're eating chicken for dinner *again* because it's the only word you know.

B. When no one understands what you say, you step closer and shout louder.

C. When the barman doesn't understand your order, you point frantically at the beer.

D. You're surrounded by locals, swapping jokes, email addresses and experiences – other travellers want to borrow your phrasebook or audio guide.

If you answered A, B, or C, you NEED Lonely Planet's language products ...

- **Lonely Planet Phrasebooks** – for every phrase you need in every language you want

- **Lonely Planet Language & Culture** – get behind the scenes of English as it's spoken around the world – learn and laugh

- **Lonely Planet Fast Talk & Fast Talk Audio** – essential phrases for short trips and weekends away – read, listen and talk like a local

- **Lonely Planet Small Talk** – 10 essential languages for city breaks

- **Lonely Planet Real Talk** – downloadable language audio guides from lonelyplanet.com to your MP3 player

... and this is why

- **Talk to everyone everywhere**
  Over 120 languages, more than any other publisher

- **The right words at the right time**
  Quick-reference colour sections, two-way dictionary, easy pronunciation, every possible subject – and audio to support it

Lonely Planet Offices

Australia
90 Maribyrnong St, Footscray,
Victoria 3011
☎ 03 8379 8000
fax 03 8379 8111
✉ talk2us@lonelyplanet.com.au

USA
150 Linden St, Oakland,
CA 94607
☎ 510 250 6400
fax 510 893 8572
✉ info@lonelyplanet.com

UK
2nd fl, 186 City Rd,
London EC1V 2NT
☎ 020 7106 2100
fax 020 7106 2101
✉ go@lonelyplanet.co.uk

lonelyplanet.com